THE LIBERTY OF
OUR LANGUAGE
REVEALED

WE BRING ABOUT WHAT WE TALK ABOUT

Thomas Blackwell

ISBN: 0692056793
ISBN-13: 978-0692056790

Manufactured in the United States of America

What Others Are Saying...

"*The Liberty of Our Language Revealed* is a must-read if you are ready to create the next best season of your life. Thomas is a master crafter of language, intention, and the power of shaping your future with the choices that you make today. I have heard him speak many times, and every time he is about to take the stage I am greeted with great anticipation yet again, knowing he will make me laugh, cause me to think, inspire my soul, and awaken my spirit."

Lisa Nichols–CEO of Motivating the Masses, Bestselling Author, and World Renowned Motivational Speaker

"*The Liberty of Our Language Revealed* could not have come at a more opportune time. Thomas Blackwell's subtitle, 'We Bring About What We Talk About,' is pure truth. The principles, premises, and philosophy of this book can indeed change our world."

Tom Ziglar–Author and proud son of Zig Ziglar

"You know how people say, 'If you are going to read only one book this year...?' I'm saying, 'IF you are going to only read one book in your lifetime, *The Liberty of Our Language Revealed* is it!' The wisdom in this book is PRICELESS . . . Thomas Blackwell truly shows us how to Change our Language, so we can Change our Lives! It's Captivating and filled with Valuable Lessons. This book is one you'll want to hand down to the next generation."

Duane Cummings–CEO of Leadercast, Author, and Founder of The Sensational Group

"The Liberty of Our Language Revealed is a MASTERPIECE! This is a book that every person, employee, or leader should read and internalize. This will go down in history as a *must read* because of the impact it will have on you and those close to you. This is a book I will have my children and team read over and over. When you finish this book, share it with your friends and family so they can experience the same incredible transformation that you will!"

Rob Shallenberger–CEO of Becoming Your Best Global Leadership, National Bestselling Author, and Former Fighter Pilot

"The Liberty of Our Language Revealed does in fact reveal the path to our personal and professional freedom through the words we choose. This book is at the top of my recommended reading list. Thomas's powerful story takes you on a journey where you learn along the way–much like life does when you pay attention. He invites us to observe and become more aware of how our words actually shape our experience, and in doing so gives us the veritable keys to the kingdom! Thomas Blackwell is one of those rare speakers who always gives the audience more than they hoped for. His extensive background, his honesty in sharing his ups and downs, and his ability to connect and deliver exactly what that audience most needs makes him the perfect keynote speaker."

Nancy Matthews–Founder of Women's Prosperity Network, International Speaker, and Bestselling Author

"There are books we read that hold the power to transform our lives. *The Liberty of Our Language Revealed* is one of them. I've had the pleasure of knowing Thomas and seeing him speak on several stages around the world over the last few years. Each time he has spoken, I've witnessed his words inspire, uplift, and impact the lives of everyone in the room. When I heard of his new book project, I was intrigued to see what it was all about. True to form, Thomas has delivered. The stories and messages shared in these pages are incredibly powerful. You will not only be inspired to grow and improve, but you will have the tools you need to go within and transform your mindset and the world around you forever."

Sean Greeley–CEO of NPE (Net Profit Explosion)

"Knowing Thomas as I have as a man, father, entrepreneur, speaker, and spiritual leader, I knew his message would be truly inspirational, and he did not disappoint at all with the *Liberty of Our Language Revealed*. I could not put it down from the moment I received the preview copy. In life our words matter, and the language we use matters. Whether we speak the words out loud to one, one thousand, or speak them to ourselves, our language has a great and lasting impact. I love the message of change your language to change your life, and everything always works out for you when you put your faith in God. The world will be a better place because of this book and very timely message."

Nicholas J. Loise–President of GKIC

"Thomas Blackwell epitomizes the use of language to create influence, change, and action among his audiences. Unlike many how to books, Thomas's brilliant use of stories is sure to leave you engaged from cover to cover while delivering the skills necessary for you to command any room, any where, anytime!"

Dr. Andreas Boettcher–The Ironman of Sales, DrAndreas.com

"Thomas's giftedness in communication and storytelling comes alive in *The Liberty of Our Language Revealed*. He takes you through a journey filled with interesting characters that provide wisdom and insight around purpose, gratitude, decision making and so much more."

Eric English–CEO of Creative Why

"The Liberty of Our Language Revealed enlightened me on a new and unique approach to the fact that our 'words matter,' and by making a few small changes, you can help change your world! This is a must–read for anyone, whether you are an individual or a leader of an organization who wants to immediately improve your results. I've been privileged to hear Thomas deliver many keynote presentations; everybody in the room is engaged and captivated from the moment he opens his mouth!"

Davy Tyburski–America's Chief Profit Officer™, ChiefProfitOfficer.com

"Thomas Blackwell delivers bigtime! Not since Og Mandino first captivated us with *The Greatest Salesman in the World* has a teacher come along with the ability to change lives through storytelling and the sharing of life experience like Thomas has done here. Get ready for a mysterious and passionate episode in a blooming speaker's life as his future is unfolded before him in a scenario he was destined to share. Destiny found the right man for *The Liberty of Our Language!*"

Kevin Allen–CEO and Founder of Listen University

"Thomas shares powerful, life-changing, yet simple truths about the liberty of language. These truths have endless potential to control your world, the life you live, and the joy you feel with language congruent to your dreams. Ennobled by the keys shared in *The Liberty of Our Language Revealed*, Thomas has become one of the most inspiring and motivational speakers of our time."

Mark Brown–CEO of Orange Sock Payment Systems

"There are people who truly understand how to help others take action and inspire them to live at a higher level . . . that is Thomas Blackwell. I have contracted Thomas to speak at many of our events, and I have had people tell me that they come to the event just to watch, learn, and be inspired by his keynote talk. I have hired him personally to train my top sales people, and they thanked me over and over. You will be thankful each and every time you engage Thomas. No matter what level that is—sharing his brilliantly written book, having him speak at your event, or doing training with him personally or with your top people."

Mike Crow–CEO of Coach Blueprint, Founder of Mastermind Inspector Community, and Magnetic Marketing Business Advisor

"Simply put, Thomas Blackwell delivers. I'm excited about *The Liberty of Our Language Revealed* because the power of the spoken word cannot be discussed enough. We are what we think, and we do what we believe. . . . I have thoroughly enjoyed working with Thomas as a speaker at my conferences; his ability to inspire, and sincere and passionate outlook on life are second to none."

Howard Partridge–International business coach, and Best-Selling author of The Power of Community - How Phenomenal Leaders Inspire their Teams, WOW their Customers and Make Bigger Profits.

A Personal Note from the Editor

In the Judeo-Christian heritage exists an often whimsically-held narrative that describes the creation of our world. "In the beginning . . . God *said*, let there be light: and there was light . . ." (see KJV Genesis 1:1, 3, 11, 14, 20, 24, 26). God's all-powerful contributions to our lives began with His words. He said, and the light and the dark, the land and the water, and the flora and fauna commenced. Literally, a place for mankind to strive and to thrive was initiated, with an utterance.

But, are we that powerful? Though it may somewhat sound like magic, perhaps that is exactly what we have been given in *The Liberty of Our Language Revealed*. A great quote, inconclusively attributed to many sources, both warns and invites us, **"Watch your thoughts; for they become words. Watch your words; for they become actions. Watch your actions; for they become habits. Watch your habits; for they become character. Watch your character; for it will become your destiny."**

During the process of reviewing the drafts for this book, I carried the principles I was learning with me in my daily walk and talk. I performed the experiments found on its pages in front of classrooms full of college students and church groups who were both mesmerized and cautioned by the "power" of our words. I shared the emotionally-charged stories with my friends, wife, and children, invoking lessons that will not soon be forgotten. I've learned to catch myself in long-held practices that weaken me, and have more confidently pursued opportunities to help others do the same.

In Aramaic, the somewhat defamed term *abracadabra* might give us a connection to the message contained in Thomas's writing. Today, if someone uses this phrase, we half-expect to see rabbit in a hat. However, its origins are not so "smoke and mirrors." Its original meaning was "it will be created in my words." Our communication is not meant to be flashy nor beguiling, but rather empowering and ennobling.

In *The Liberty of Our Language Revealed*, Thomas has shared his heart and soul with us, the readers. As a big fan and a friend, and knowing what he is made of, I will be the first to add that what he has given us represents a precious gift, one "that keeps on giving." Our receipt of this gift will be left up to us. Learn to say what you mean and mean what you say, so that you too can begin to feel the majesty, power, and liberty of your own language.

Speak well,

C. Ryan Dunn, Ph.D.

Contents

CONTENTS

Foreword
By David Bayer

There was something different the first time I heard Thomas Blackwell speak. Thomas's story is truly inspiring. A story of extraordinary professional, personal, and spiritual achievement despite the kinds of challenges and hardship that limit most peoples' lives. His sharp wit and sense of humor, coupled with his generous humility, made it nearly impossible to resist a feeling of kinship and friendship with a man I had first seen on stage that day. But on that day when I first heard him speak, these were not the qualities that made Thomas something and someone truly different to me. What powerfully set Thomas apart from the hundreds of other speakers I've heard and seen over the years was the intentionality of his language.

I don't know how much of the storyline from *The Liberty of Our Language Revealed* is truth or fiction. Nor do I think that really matters much. What I do know is that the character of Thomas Blackwell *is* the Thomas Blackwell that I've been blessed to know. "Hi David, how incredible are you?" Thomas will ask when we speak by phone. In any environment and in any situation, Thomas intentionally creates and influences the energy of every interaction. I believe that each of us represents a concept, a mission, a reason, or an idea whose time it is to be brought into the world. Who Thomas is and his big idea are absolutely clear to anyone who has experienced his presence: what we talk about, we bring about.

Our state of being dictates our destiny. When we are joyful, we bring more joy in to the world. When we are certain, we create more certainty. When we are intentional, we get from life what we intended. And, if there is a single, indicative guidepost to how we are feeling, what we are thinking, and what we are creating, it is that which we speak. Perhaps even more powerfully, what we say also influences the way we and the way others feel. In *The Liberty of Our Language Revealed*, Thomas

Blackwell shares a set of core principles to help each and every one of us become more powerful creators through an awareness and a conscious, intentional use of our Creator's gift of language. As you read, understand, and begin to implement the framework of language outlined in this book, you will unlock a new potential and a new reality in every area of your life. *The Liberty of Our Language Revealed* isn't just a story, it is a manual. A manual for understanding and mastering the power contained within the laws of language. It is a once-in-a-generation book that has the capacity to set you free. Will this book be that for you? As our dear friend Thomas would say, it will "if you say so!"

Sincerely,

David Bayer—Creator of "The Powerful Living Experience" and Author of *Mind Hack*

To Kimberly, Makayla, Charity, Melody June, & Liberty May

. . . the book that set us free.

Introduction

Why, The Liberty of Our Language Revealed?

I have thought long and hard on why I should write a book that reveals the truth, **"what we talk about we bring about,"** Why speak to people around the world about paying attention to the words that come out of our mouths? Why write a book about changing our language in order to change our lives? Hasn't it all been said already? Haven't there already been books, movies, and documentaries about this matter?

Doesn't everyone plainly understand that when we change our language we change our results? Isn't everyone already living their dreams, and experiencing a completely fulfilled life? Doesn't the human race know that we have the power to verbally command our future into what we really want? Isn't it clear already that some of the most powerful movements in history are because of something someone said? Don't people, especially athletes, already know how to talk to themselves in order to secure the victory? Isn't it obvious that if a CEO or manager wants to get the best out of his/her people, superior language is necessary? Isn't it common sense to do more doing than thinking? I am sure everyone already wakes up in the morning, has their day planned, and repeat all the positive things that are going to take place in their lives, right? Everyone is already an expert on how whatever we focus on and talk about expands, aren't they? By now surely everyone understands that people tend to act how you speak to them, wouldn't you say?

When I came to a strong realization that the above questions were not commonplace and the answers were not rhetorical, I decided to create *The Liberty of Our Language*

Revealed. Inside this book you will get crystal clear on how to change your language in order to change your life. The law of attraction truly comes to fruition when the chosen words come out of your mouth. Whether it is what you want or what you don't want, either way it comes to pass.

In a way I grew a little weary of asking people if they had heard about the Law of Attraction, because they were still not attracting the things they really wanted in life. How do I know, you ask? It's simple: **because they said so.** Their language was not congruent with what they really wanted. When your words, conversations, prayers, vocabulary, and even karaoke performances are on the same page as your true desires, you will discover the missing gems in your life that were essentially there all along. Our words are actually the golden key that unlocks the sought-after treasure.

The way I hear it, many of us need to make some language and mindset improvements. Some major and some minor. You will come to know what those are for you as you read and **apply** the **lessons learned** inside this book. This is a journey I've taken to a higher standard in my own life, and I am sincerely grateful and excited you have decided to join me.

The vision of this book and movement is to **significantly improve the language and mindset of more than one billion people worldwide.**

You should know that *The Liberty of Our Language Revealed* is a fictional story I created based on actual events and experiences that have occurred in my life and history. Many phrases and words will be highlighted throughout the story with the intention that you will implement them in your daily language.

There will also be occasional **{Power Paragraphs}** noted

that should be considered for immediate application.

You should also know that everything I am and everything I have of worth is because of the Lord. As you receive inspirational impressions on things you should change for the better, please know those feelings are not from me as the author. Those feelings come from that Source that is infinitely greater than us all, One who desires our happiness and well-being in all aspects of our lives. I have sought His guidance to write this book. This is the same way I seek His direction every time I am asked to speak to an audience somewhere. The Lord knows you personally as the reader, He knows the audience that is listening, and only He can cause a stirring in your heart and mind regarding the positive changes that need to happen in your life.

Okay my friend, are you ready to get started? . . . **If you say so!**

Chapter 1

The Contest

     In a few minutes it would be my turn to give a speech for the contest I had reluctantly entered. A few months ago, the ad in the magazine read, "Speech Contest, $10,000 Prize and a Chance to Change the World". I was not sure what "a chance to change the world" meant, but I was pretty clear about the ten thousand dollars.

     Up to this point, I had spoken to groups of people nearly every week for more than seven years, inspiring them to get their financial houses in order and to potentially join my team of agents. The feeling of confidence to enter such a contest was borrowed from a select few who claimed that public speaking is a path I should take. So there I was on borrowed confidence and a great deal of hope that somehow, some way this speech contest would spark my newfound speaking career.

     It was decided that my wife, Kimberly, would stay at home in Montpelier, Virginia, with our three girls while I traveled to Boston for the contest. Her last words to me still ring in my heart as she dropped me off at the airport: "I believe in you." Thirteen years earlier, she was my high school sweetheart; now I was watching her drive away with our three daughters.

My oldest daughters, Makayla and Charity, each made me a special card with hearts and kisses on them to wish me luck. As I watched their hands frantically wave good-byes out of the car windows, I was overwhelmed with the evident blessings in my life.

Entering the contest was a big leap of faith for me, and I was quite apprehensive. I had built a fairly successful business, and it was tempting to just continue on with it and not pursue public speaking. However, I also felt it was time to pursue a rising passion and make a shift. I determined the only way to move forward was to go for it, despite my apprehension.

Due to my last-minute registration, the hotel where the contest was being held was fully booked, and I was summoned to alternative lodging. The website said it was a two star accommodation; after my stay, I would give it half a star on a good day. I think the TV in my room came straight from the "I Love Lucy" era. It sure would have been nice to stay at the luxurious hotel where the contest was being held; nonetheless, I was thankful to be there and grateful my contest application was accepted.

It was the beginning of December and the air was crisp and cool outside, but snow had not arrived yet. While in the cheap hotel my mind reflected on the rich things in my life. Our youngest daughter had been born a month before; ironically, we felt impressed to name her Liberty. Kimberly and I delivered her alone at home in our bathtub, of all places. The unassisted birth was a singular experience, and certainly not as hard or daunting as some people may imagine. That hallowed feeling when I held our little angel in my arms for the first time earned a permanent place in my heart. God knew our situation, and the blessing Liberty would be to us. A little more than a year before Liberty was born we had another precious daughter. We knew her name should be Melody June. As it was supposed to be, even though it was not as we had planned, after just thirteen days, our little sweetheart returned to heaven. Now, having another baby to hold was a choice blessing for us. Someone once reflected, "The best way to have a piece of heaven in your home is to have someone from your home in heaven." That certainly made more sense to me now.

Once my contest entry was accepted, I was given the topic of "perspective"; I had to deliver it in front of an audience in five minutes or less. I figured the best thing to do was to tell a good story and make a point. I estimated approximately 150 people in the crowd filling the seats of the historic ballroom, including a panel of five judges. I glanced at the critical audience, half of which were contestants, each one with what I believed to be an undermining hope that I would stumble over my selected words.

Everyone had the same non-emotional introduction, including first and last name and the title of the speech, at which point the crowd was instructed to clap. "Here we go," I winced as the announcer said, "Our next speaker is Thomas Blackwell, and his speech is entitled 'Changing our Perspective'." I had spoken to audiences so many times before, but for some reason this one felt a lot more intimidating. I nervously shuffled to the center of the stage, beheld the crowd, and mustered up a smile. All eyes were on me; it was go time and the moment to deliver what I had prepared. As I stood there in front of the microphone I was enveloped with both a last-minute surge of confidence as well as inexplicable terror. *What have I gotten myself into?* I unproductively thought. Finally, the words were apprehensively released from my lips.

{Talk Given at the Speech Contest}

I grew up in a small town. Sometimes in small towns there can be certain perspectives that have been embedded in the people. One of those paradigms was about a young man about age twenty named Simpson. You see, Simpson was not your typical twenty-year-old. He looked normal, he was tall and well built, but he was mentally challenged. Most of the time, he was on his bike cruising around town. Everyone knew who Simpson was and that he was essentially harmless. Nevertheless, our parents always told us to stay away from Simpson, because, "you never know what he might do."

I was six years old when that perspective changed. One day my two older brothers and I had been playing in an irrigation channel that had a very strong current. It ran about 150 yards in length, and then it went underground. There were two ladders at each end of the channel. We thought it would be fun to climb down the ladder on one end, let the water explosively take us down, then grab on to the ladder at the other end. The current was extremely powerful; standing up would be near impossible for us. We knew this because, like any intelligent kids, we decided to test the waters by pushing a huge bolder in the raging channel just to get an idea of how powerful it really was. When we saw that the almost-immovable bolder was rushed away like a plastic bag in a windstorm, we got excited at the prospect . . . ironically.

We also put a lot of research and development into this human circus act by tying a sturdy rope on each ladder to grab on to for extra support. C'mon—you think we'd be crazy enough just to rely on the ladder? Not these three genius brothers. Now, if you happened to miss the ladder or the rope at the other end, the result was death. Other than that, it looked like a good time.

(I was a little more hopeful once the audience blurted out a string of laughter.)

My oldest brother, Wick, was the first to give it a shot; he successfully grabbed the ladder at the end of the channel before it went underground. Next it was Garrett's turn, who was just two years older than me. There he went, racing down the vicious channel, but when he got to the other side he lost his grip and fell back in the current. My heart sank, and I screamed in terror as I was about to witness my brother being swept away into an irretrievable abyss of irrigation water. There was nothing we could do. We knew we would be easily swept away if we tried to save him.

(I paused to let the audience soak in the very real possibility of a disastrous outcome.)

It was one of those times you hope and pray that God intervenes and sends a guardian angel. Well, I will never forget that God did send an angel that day. Without our noticing, Simpson, the twenty-year-old mentally handicapped hero, was somehow there at the end of the channel. He wasn't there before, but miraculously he was there now. With no hesitation, he got off his bike, jumped down into the irrigation channel, stood up in the ferocious water, caught my brother before he was swept underground forever, and put him back on dry land. Then he just got on his bike and rode away as if nothing had happened.

(I paused again to allow the listeners to experience that sense of triumph.)

My oldest brother and I just stood there, in awe of what had just taken place. We then realized we couldn't find Garrett anywhere. Then we heard, "Psst—hey guys," coming from the cotton field across the street. We quickly found out that the situation was much more precarious than we had expected. The current was so strong it pulled my brother's shorts right off; he was now naked and hiding in the cotton field. I distinctly remember that the thought of having to tell Mom that we were playing in a dangerous irrigation channel, and that her son was now naked as a result, seemed more serious than telling her he'd almost drowned. That's the perspective of a six-year-old for you. (The audience roared with laughter.) Of course, my oldest brother devised a plan with two options: One, to have me give Garrett my shorts and then ride home on my bicycle in my undies; or, two, I ride home and get some particulars for him while he hid in the cotton field. I chose option two, having previously experienced option one. Either way, Mom was destined to find out, and . . . she did.

Well after that experience, whenever we boys left the house to play, my Mom would say, "Make sure to take Simpson with you!" She obviously gained a new perspective about Simpson, as did many people in that small town. Almost overnight our new friend, who was previously considered a potentially dangerous nuisance, was now accepted and respected. Yet part of me was a little sad that all that time was lost and wasted on false beliefs about Simpson.

I hope we will base our perspective of people, groups, companies, or organizations on our personal experience with them, and not simply succumb to what everyone else may ignorantly believe. You never know when someone's life might be saved as a result of it. Thank you.

As I closed my remarks, I stood there anticipating a response from the crowd for what seemed to be an eternity. I glanced over at the panel of judges and noticed that a couple of them were overcome by emotion, or maybe they were just appalled that an inexperienced individual like me would dare enter such a contest. Suddenly and without warning, the audience and fellow contestants burst into applause. I acknowledged their reaction with a genuine smile and exited the stage as instructed.

During the other speeches that followed mine, my body was present but my mind was elsewhere; wondering whether I could win the contest and what effect it would have on my life. When the last speaker was finished, the judges announced that they would debate behind closed doors for about an hour, after which time they would announce the winner.

To date, that may have been the longest hour of my life. The anxiety weighed heavy. I needed to walk, breathe, and settle down. I was more nervous than before I stepped onto the stage to speak. I escaped to the only retreat available, the men's restroom. I furiously splashed water on my face and spoke self-directed words of encouragement. Suddenly, a man next to me appeared in the mirror. With water still on my face and skewing my sight, I couldn't make out his face very well. Besides, there is an unwritten rule that men do not make eye contact in the bathroom.

"You were the best one today," he said, his back now toward me as he exited.

I quickly wiped the water from my face and looked to see if anyone else was in the restroom. It was empty; was he talking to me? "Thank you," I said softly, not wanting to be accused of talking to myself in the men's restroom.

Back in the banquet hall, the dreaded time had arrived to listen to the judges' decision. On the outside I was calm and collected; however, on the inside my body was in a frenzy.

"We would like to thank all of you who entered the contest,

and to the audience who attended today," one of the judges explained from the stage. "We must say how impressed we were with all of the speeches," he continued. His words were emphatically slow, as if intentionally calculated to drag out the already unbearable suspense. The tension grew among the speakers. There could only be one winner. No second prize. This was it: either I win, or I go home none the richer–in fact, out the cost of my one-star hotel. The words from the gentleman in the bathroom rang in my head over and over, "You were the best one today!" Finally the judge concluded, "The winner of the ninth annual speech contest is . . . Thomas Blackwell!"

I sat somewhat paralyzed. I wasn't sure how to react– whether to jump for joy or simply start crying. I believed it was possible for me to win or I wouldn't have entered the contest, but somehow I managed to brew up a feeling of unbelief that I actually won! I seemed to be the only one sitting as an electrifying standing ovation broke out among the participants and supporters to congratulate me. As I gathered my emotions I approached the stage where the judge, acting as voice, congratulated me. I was beyond a handshake and eagerly embraced the judge who announced my name. A bit surprised that I hugged him, he handed me an envelope and whispered to me, "Open this envelope only when you are certain you are alone." He then motioned to the microphone, and the crowd humorously erupted, "Speech, speech, speech!"

The floor was once again mine to say something, but this time I had no prepared comments. The room fell graciously silent. I gazed out and observed a few tears in some of my fellow contestant's eyes. It was clear the tears were not for me, rather the inner emotion that comes when you put your heart into something, do your best, sacrifice in unshared ways, and yet fall short of the desired prize. With this sobering realization the words began to come to me.

"Thank you for putting this contest together; I am sincerely grateful for this honor," I said humbly as I peered at the judges. Now pointing my attention to the audience, I continued, "I was thinking maybe I should just split the check among all of us, but then I thought of my poor division skills and decided it would be easier on everyone if I just kept the money myself." It was my attempt to lighten the mood a bit.

(A trickle of laughter seemed to open their minds to listen to what I was about to say.)

"Winning a contest certainly does not determine whether we are winners or losers. Winning comes with the fact that we all had the courage to submit a registration and show up. Winning comes with how we decide to handle the results of the contest. As I heard you all speak from this same stage, I learned from you, I was inspired by you, and I am a better person because of what you said. I honestly don't know why I was selected, and I am sure it was quite a chore for the judges to come to this conclusion. My hope is that this day is a beginning for all of us. So I would like to congratulate us all for winning the unseen victories we have achieved just for being here."

I confidently stepped back from the microphone and directed my applause at the audience. Another standing ovation trickled throughout the crowd, but this time, it was not designed for me.

Chapter 2

The Sealed Envelope

The money did not seem as valuable as the overwhelming feeling of joy that came upon me as I received the standing ovation; nevertheless, I was unquestionably grateful for it. Through all the excitement and congratulations, I was intrigued when the judge told me to open the sealed envelope only when certain I was alone.

I was so excited to call my biggest fans: Kimberly and my sweet little girls. "We did it", I said softly to the love of my life. A huge uproar of enthusiasm exploded from the other end of the phone. I have always said that my wife gets excited enough for both of us; she has trained our daughters to show extreme enthusiasm also. Kimberly began to cry, we said a prayer of gratitude over the phone. I told her about the sealed envelope and that I needed to find a place where no one was around so I could open it. We exchanged a tender "I love you" and I promised to call her later, as soon as I found out for myself what all of this meant.

It was almost like I became an instant celebrity. Everywhere I turned, someone recognized me. I was trying to scout out a place for some privacy in the lobby, but to no avail. I gazed upward at the incredible vaulted ceilings and the masterful craftsmanship; unfortunately the happy thoughts vanished as I thought of the indecent cheap hotel I was returning to that night.

As I went out into the courtyard, I started toward a bench where I knew I could inconspicuously open the envelope. I looked around and took in the impressive structure of the historic hotel. I learned that it was recently renovated; prior to this, it had been the Charles Street jail for more than 135 years. I further learned that it had housed several famous inmates, such as Malcom X; Ferdinando Sacco; Bartolomeo Vanzetti; and former governor and multi-term mayor of Boston, James Michael Hurley. Some of the rooms, and definitely the restaurant, had some of the original prison preserved.

I focused on the envelope one more time. I carefully opened the seal to find a neatly handwritten note wrapped around a check for ten thousand dollars. I took a deep breath and just starred at it for a minute. I'd been speaking for years per se, but this was my first direct compensation. My confidence began to build that just maybe this whole notion of speaking for as a vocation would work. I reflected on all the countless hours invested in self-development, running organizations, memorizing powerful quotes, and fanatically studying the habits of successful people. For years, the time spent driving my car and mowing my lawn have been a self-development academy, as I listen to audio books of high achievers.

I took another glance at the check, then curiously began to read the personal note.

"Dear Thomas,

Congratulations on your recent victory. An executive suite has been reserved for you at this Hotel for as many nights as you desire. Furthermore, a very important meeting has been arranged for you to meet someone who will help you with your chance to change the world. Tonight at 11:00 p.m. sharp you are to report in the basement for further instructions. Again, we congratulate you."

My heart raced as I wondered about this meeting. I went to the registration desk, now as a guest, and inquired, "My name is Thomas Blackwell and I believe you have a suite reserved for me?"

"Of course, Mr. Blackwell, we are honored to have you stay in our luxurious hotel," the lady answered as if I were some eminent guest. She handed me the room key, and I headed to the elevator.

While in the elevator, I noticed there were no buttons to go down to the basement; the first floor was the lowest level listed. I briefly thought about it and concluded that there must be some other access besides the elevator. I did not think much about it as I anticipated what my suite was going to look like.

My jaw dropped as I entered the 2200-square-foot suite. I had never stayed in a room so magnificent. I could see the Charles River and the Back Bay skyline from the inside. I had my own private terrace that overlooked the city. I sat in one of the patio chairs and just soaked it all in—the contest, the standing ovation, the money, the note . . . Oh no, the note! I panicked! I glanced at my watch and suddenly remembered my

11:00 meeting in the basement. It was 10:45, and I needed to be early to make a good impression.

I got off the elevator at the first floor. *The basement, the basement,* I kept telling myself, *where in the world is that basement?* I rushed over to the registration desk to inquire of the same lady who gave me my key.

"Can you tell me how to get to the basement?"

She stepped back from the counter with a puzzled look and said, "I am sorry, Mr. Blackwell, but the hotel does not have a basement." My stomach dropped. Many terrifying thoughts scattered through my head at once. Had I been deceived? Was this some sort of game? Maybe it was a challenge.

Once again, I focused on the registration desk attendant, "Excuse me, Miss, can I speak to your manager for a moment?"

Soon the manager was there to help me, but when he arrived he quickly confirmed what I was told before. "I am sorry, Mr. Blackwell, our hotel does not have a basement. Can I help you with anything else?"

"No, thanks," I quickly responded. By now, my mind was spinning. Why would they tell me to meet in the basement if no such location existed? I looked at my watch. It was 10:52 p.m. I had eight minutes to figure out where this basement was, or what it meant.

Staff members at the registration desk were whispering to each other, watching to see my next move. I went back to the elevators and saw the fire escape. I jerked the door open to see if the stairs led down to the mysterious basement. My stomach sank even further as the tragic reality stared me in the face: no stairs going down. I regrouped my thoughts. *What in the world is going on? I will not give up until I find this basement.* It was time to stop depending on myself and to call on a Higher Power. From boyhood, my father instilled in me a divine habit to always call on God for help. I closed my eyes and took a few deep breaths.

In my mind, I asked, *Where do I need to go in order to find the basement?* A clear thought came to my mind, "Go to the restaurant downstairs." Determined and hopeful, I quickly walked down the escalator and my eyes were fixed on a bar and lounge on the bottom floor of the hotel.

The hostess's podium was left unattended; the bartender blurted out without looking at me, "Restaurant closes at 11:00 and the bar is open until 2:00 a.m." I just nodded, barely acknowledging him; I walked past the bar and looked into the rooms that had once been jail cells but that were now filled with tables and chairs. The restaurant was empty, and the lights were being turned off. I walked into the first jail cell; I searched for some sort of fake wall or trap door but could not find anything. I immediately moved on to the center cell, but no such luck. The lights were off in the restaurant as it was now closed; somehow, no one saw me snooping around. Only one more possibility, if indeed a clue to the basement existed. I walked into the third cell, holding my cell phone up to provide some light; suddenly, the cast iron gate closed behind me. A silhouette was standing in the doorway.

"I am impressed you found it," said a somewhat familiar voice.

A little shaken and confused, I muttered, "What is going on?"

"Are you ready for a chance to change the world?" the man said softly, not wanting anyone to know we were in the restaurant.

"What do you mean change the—"

"Yes or no," he promptly cut me off.

I paused. Somehow something inside made me want to commit to whatever this mysterious person asked of me. "Yes," I affirmed.

He nodded his head and with a low clear voice said, "You were the best one today." He was now moving out of the shadow toward me. I still did not recognize his face.

"My name is Clemson Wright, but people I trust call me Clem," he whispered as he walked to the corner of the former jail cell.

Clemson slid the far right corner table quietly to the left and likewise moved the chairs out of the way. I was now standing right next to him; I felt a tingle run down my spine as we both gazed at what looked like a hidden cellar door that was situated exactly in the spot where the table had been. He reached down and slid the metal door to the side, unveiling a small opening that led down somewhere with an old wooden ladder to facilitate the descent.

"Follow me," he commanded. A little hesitant, I looked back at the empty restaurant to see if anyone was looking. I thought of my wife and girls back home; how was I going to explain this to Kimberly? I turned and looked down at the small hole cut into the floor, realizing I had committed to something much bigger than I had anticipated. I made my way down behind Clemson. Each step I took creaked as my weight alternated down the rungs of the old wooden ladder. As soon as I was low enough, I slid the door back over the opening as I was instructed.

My heart was racing now as I followed Clemson down a dark hallway save the light from his cell phone. No wonder the hotel manager said there was no basement—so far as he or anyone else was aware, there *was* no basement. As we progressed through the hallway, I noticed several phrases carved on the walls, but we were moving too fast to be able to make them out, and I did not want to get too far behind Clemson. He appeared to be in great shape and well built as he briskly walked down the hallway. He looked to be in his early fifties—dark brown hair with a few grey streaks, clean shaven with a square face. The air smelled of old wood and dusty cement walls. Suddenly, the hallway opened up into a large dark space. He flicked a match and lit an old kerosene lantern. My eyes peered slowly around the room, taking in all of the writings on the walls.

"What is this place?" I inquired of Clemson.

"Welcome to the escape route dug out by many of the inmates while serving time at the Charles Street jail," he declared. Another tingle went up my spine.

"How many people know about it?" I asked hesitantly.

"Alive, just three . . . You, my father, and me," he replied.

"Why are we down here, Clemson? What's going on?" I asked quizzically, coming to grips with the fact that no one else on the planet knew my whereabouts.

"Relax, Thomas, and by the way, you can call me Clem," he said, comforting my fears and letting me know he trusted me.

"Let me explain a few things to you Mr. Blackwell. We have held this speech contest every year for the past nine years;

each contest winner was asked to meet me in the basement at precisely 11:00 p.m. for a chance to change the world. Out of all the contest winners, you are the only one who ever found it. The winners who have preceded you asked the manager of the hotel about the basement, just as you probably did; but unlike you, they decided to believe that there was no basement." His language was direct and assertive, yet his tone felt congratulatory. "Thomas, I am curious to know why it is you persisted looking for the basement?"

I paused for a moment before I answered; I was trying to gather my thoughts. "When I was told there was no basement, I was a little flustered, to be honest," I replied. "I guess I have learned in my life that when someone tells you 'no,' or when they say that something is not possible, I can decide to believe it or I can find out for myself. To answer your question, Mr. Wright, I decided to find out for myself if there really was a basement, regardless of what the hotel manager said."

There was silence in the old musky room. Clem seemed satisfied with my response as he silently nodded his head with approval. He broke the silence and continued his inquiry, "Thomas, I am very interested to find out how it is you knew to come to the restaurant?"

For a brief instant, I was tempted to credit myself with the idea to go to the hotel restaurant; however I knew this was not the case. Like a good angel on my right shoulder encouraging me, I recalled the well-known words from William Shakespeare, **"To thine own self be true."**

Softly, I started, "After I did everything I could possibly do myself . . ."

I paused, not knowing if Clem believed in the power of prayer or even if he believed in God. I took a breath of confidence and simply said, "I said a prayer and asked God where the basement was; I had a clear impression to come to the restaurant. I walked in the restaurant even though I was told it was closed, and that's where I met you, for the second time."

"The second time?" Clem probed.

"Wasn't it you I saw in the bathroom?" I stammered.

"Yeah, that was me," he said jokingly. Clem smiled, satisfied with my answers and said, "I knew that whoever dug deep enough and sought higher knowledge, or insight, would eventually find the basement." I felt peace come over me, knowing I had said what was in my heart, thereby expressing my true character.

Mr. Wright walked to the corner of the room and picked up a wooden box. From inside the box, he pulled out an old, worn-out book. Stuffed in the back of the binding were several pieces of paper filled with hand-written notes. Clem pulled out the notes and handed me the book. The book appeared to have been sitting in that box for many years. The title was carved into the dried-up leather cover by some sort of nail or perhaps a knife.

I read the title: *The Liberty of Our Language Revealed.*

"You ever heard of it before?" Clem inquired.

"No, I haven't," I answered, opening its dusty pages. "Wait, these pages are blank, and there is no author!" I declared, as I flipped back to the front cover to see if any name was written.

Clem paused and made eye contact with me, "You are the author, Thomas; you are the author of *The Liberty of Our Language Revealed.*"

I paced back and forth staring at the empty book in my hand. "Clem, I have never written a book before; why would I be the person to do it? I don't know if I even understand what it is supposed to be about. Why are you so sure I am the guy to write it?" I questioned, a little overwhelmed with the prospects of being an author. "Is this what my chance to change the world is, a dusty old book?" I continued.

Clem kept quiet with his arms folded, and he seemed to be enjoying my frustration. "It's a chance to change the world if you want and allow it to be. What I need to know is whether you are the right person to do it," he replied, with a little more force than I was accustomed to. "You have proven that you can inspire a small crowd with your speaking abilities, but can you author a worldwide movement?" he continued.

"That's what this is, Thomas, a movement to help people truly change their lives and enjoy the success they deserve!" Clem said passionately.

"Look, Clem, why don't you write the book?" I asked softly, attempting to calm the energy in the room.

"That's not what I was instructed to do," he stated.

"Instructed by whom?" I inquired.

"I will let you know if you accept the responsibility to be the author and mouthpiece for *The Liberty of Our Language Revealed*. Let's cut to the chase, Mr. Blackwell, do I have the right person for this movement or not?"

This was not a decision I wanted to make on my own. "Clem, can you give me just a minute?" I asked.

"You have exactly sixty seconds to give me your answer," he responded firmly.

I turned around and walked quickly into to the dark hallway. I took a deep breath. The musky, desolate air filled my senses with a deepened awareness that something significant happened in this old escape route. Something was waiting to be awakened for the good of mankind; was it my calling to do it? For me there was only one way to find out, and if it is my path I would never doubt again. I would grant it all the effort I possessed. *God, is this what I am supposed to do? Is this my mission at hand—to inspire people and help them change their language, so they can change their lives and enjoy the success they deserve? I feel like I can do it, but is this what I am supposed to be doing?* I inquired in my mind and heart. As I stood there, a gradual feeling of warmth and peace encircled me, confirming that it was the right thing to do.

I walked back into the room with no more hesitation and said, "I will do it."

"Fifty-seven seconds," Clemson Wright said, almost cutting me off while looking down at his watch.

Chapter 3

The Instructions

"I have a few things to explain to you. You'll probably want to sit down for this," declared Clem while handing me the old wooden box that once contained the book.

"My full name is Clemson James Michael Wright," he said in a steady, soft tone as if I was supposed to know the meaning of it. Clem paced the room with both hands in his pockets as I sat on the little box feeling a bit like I was watching a tennis match, side to side.

He continued, "I am telling you this because it is important for you to know where that name came from. My great-grandfather, Walter Wright, was a postman for several years. His family struggled financially; he was not fortunate enough to have a lot of schooling growing up. He was a working-class man. My great-grandfather learned of a job opening with the government; the wages would be four times his mailman salary. A requirement for the position was a test—some sort of civil service exam from what I was told. The day came for the exam and that's when Walter Wright met Mayor

James Michael Hurley," Clem explained.

"Wait, was that the same James Michael Hurley who was an inmate here at the Charles Street jail?" I asked curiously.

"Precisely," he answered, determined to continue the story. "Walter Wright met the mayor in the hallway of the city council building, just before he was supposed to take the civil service exam. Mayor Hurley took an interest in my great-grandfather; the mayor could sense his anxiety and fear of failing the exam. And that's when it happened."

"That's when what happened, Clem?" I eagerly asked while sitting on the edge of that little wooden box.

Clem continued, "The mayor walked to the administrative desk and requested a copy of the civil service exam so he could review it. He brought the written document into the hallway where my great-grandfather was still seated and filled in all the answers for him. Needless to say, Walter Wright got the government job after acing the civil service exam," Clem said proudly.

"So, the mayor essentially took the exam for him to ensure that your great-grandfather would get the job?" I asked.

"That's exactly right, and it changed my family's financial situation and standing in the community overnight. Somehow, the incident later became public and Mayor Hurley was sentenced to jail; he fell victim to that dark reputation and was no longer courted by those in more respectable circles," Clem continued.

"As for my great-grandfather and our family, Mayor James Michael Hurley is revered as a hero, and thus the significance of my middle name." I sat in silence and absorbed this confidential information, waiting for Clem to divulge the rest of the story.

"My great-grandfather was so grateful for Mayor Hurley's help on the civil service exam that he visited the mayor almost daily here at the jail. Many times, he would bring along his son—my grandfather, Maxwell Wright—to visit the mayor. There was a reason the visits were so regular." Clem softened his voice, peering at the dark opening to the hallway making sure we were still alone.

I remained still and quiet as Clem carefully positioned his thoughts. "James Michael Hurley and a few other inmates were placed in the cell you and I entered tonight—or last night, I guess," Clem said, looking at his watch and realizing it was after midnight. "While they were in the jail cell, and unbeknownst to anyone, they began to dig out this escape route. My great-grandfather and his son were entrusted with their escape plot, and actually helped somewhat to facilitate it," Clem divulged, again looking at the dark, empty hallway.

"How was the escape route never discovered?" I asked.

"I asked my father the same thing," Clem answered. "The inmates would simply place one of their metal cots over the hole with their sheets hanging down, and miraculously, it was never discovered."

"So, did they escape!" I blurted out impatiently.

"The mayor was released early, and the other inmates were transferred, so there was never an opportunity or a need. The hole was covered up until it was . . ." Clem hesitated before telling me the next part.

"Until it was what, Clem?" I asked intently. Once again, he glanced at the dark hallway as if he was expecting someone to enter the undiscovered room without notice.

"Until it was uncovered again by my grandfather, Maxwell Wright," Clem whispered.

Suddenly, the room was pitch black. The lantern had run out of fuel. We both took out our cell phones and used them to light the room. "Should we get out of here, Clem?" I asked, not wanting to admit I was growing a little uneasy about the whole situation.

"I was instructed to give you all of this information down here. So, we need to get through this here, tonight," he answered.

Still sitting on the little wooden box, I reviewed in my mind what I had been told so far. "Wait, how did your grandfather get access to the jail cell, because the only way he could have uncovered the escape route would be if . . ."

"He was an inmate," Clem finished the sentence for me. I felt another shiver go up and down my spine. I kept quiet as I waited for him to finish the rest of the story.

Clem started again, "Maxwell Wright got a first-class education; he pursued a doctorate in communications with an emphasis in German. He eventually became a professor of communications at Boston University. It was 1945 and WWII was over, but enemy lines were still very sensitive. A German U-boat, U-234, surrendered, and its high-ranking officials were housed here at the jail. In learning of their arrival, my grandfather came to visit the German prisoners, wanting to speak with them and get a taste of their authentic language. He came often, and unfortunately was accused of treason. Because the war had just ended and German relations were still sensitive, my grandfather too was locked up. Coincidentally or fortunately, he was locked up in the exact jail cell where James Michael Hurley was held when Maxwell was just a boy."

"So, your grandpa uncovered the escape route to get out of jail and take the Germans with him?" I inquired, full of assumption.

"Not quite," Clem corrected. "My grandfather never had any intentions of escaping; he knew his stay here would be only temporary. He and some other German inmates dug out the hallway and the room we are now in to store the information in the box you are now sitting on."

I felt the wooden box underneath me with a much deeper appreciation of how it arrived. "Dr. Maxwell Wright dedicated the better part of his life to studying language and how we communicate. While he was incarcerated, he wrote several pages of notes on the power of our words," Clem explained.

"Those were your grandpa's notes in the back of the book?" I questioned.

"Yes, you're sitting on them," he added with humor in his voice. "My grandfather intended to write a book called *The Liberty of Our Language Revealed* to help people realize that what we talk about, we bring about; however, he was never able to retrieve the notes that he stored in this escape route. He was released unexpectedly and did not divulge the information of this room to anyone except my father, me, and now you."

Clem paused to let me absorb what I had just been told. "My grandfather entrusted the information to my father with a promise to one day figure out a way to retrieve his notes and get the intended message out to the world. My grandfather's life was cut short, and he passed away less than a year after being released from jail. My father and I decided to include someone else in getting the message out—someone who has a gift of speaking and inspiring people," Clem stated.

"Thomas, do you realize it has been more than fifty years since my grandpa died? When we learned that the Charles Street jail was going to be turned into a hotel, we devised a plan to get down here and find the right person. Following the opening of this hotel in 2007, we decided to hold an annual speech contest; you already know the eight other winners were not the right people, or they would have found the basement before you did," he noted again.

"Clem, is your father still alive?" I wondered.

"Yes, and you actually already met him," he answered, amused by my ignorance.

"When did I meet him?" I questioned.

"My dad announced you as the winner of the contest and gave you the sealed envelope; he was the head judge," Clemson concluded.

I stood up with the hardened leather-bound book in my hands; I opened the wooden box that had been serving as my stool for the last hour or so. I carefully handled the notes written by Dr. Maxwell Wright with a much deeper appreciation thanks to the understanding of their origin. I skimmed through the pages, and counted nine of them. Sliding them into the back binding of the book with the empty pages, I asked, "Is there anything else I need to know Clem, or can we get out of here now?"

"We can go after I show you one more thing in the hallway," he replied, motioning for me to follow him. On the walls of the hallway someone had etched several phrases. I studied each one.

"Change your language, change your life."
"Improve your results, create a better environment."
"Increase your productivity, transform your economy."
"Elevate your performance, achieve higher standards."

The phrases that were etched on the wall resonated in my head as I followed Clem back down the abandoned escape route. It was all very fascinating—the escape route, Mayor Hurley, Clem's grandfather.

"We cannot let anyone know we were down here," Clem whispered to me interrupting the conversation in my head.

We had arrived at the old wooden ladder we had used to descend from the restaurant. Clem gently moved the metal door open. Fortunately it was still dark in the restaurant, so we both climbed up and placed the table and chairs in their original places.

"We have to go out the back door of the restaurant. Otherwise we risk someone seeing us and asking too many questions," Clem explained.

We inconspicuously hurried into the kitchen and out the back door. The smell of the dumpster immediately overwhelmed my senses.

"Okay I will talk to you tomorrow to let you know where your first speaking assignment is going to be," Clem said, beginning to quickly walk away from me.

"Wait, speaking assignment? What speaking assignment?" I asked.

"I will tell you all about it tomorrow. Just meet me in the

attic of the hotel at 10:00 a.m.," he said laughingly, now a good distance from me as he continued to walk away.

"That's not funny, Clem!" I yelled, sharing in his humor, and then he was gone into the night.

I took another crippling whiff of the dumpster, and although the smell was nauseating I just stood there overwhelmed with all the events that had taken place. "Wait, surely there is not an attic in the hotel," I said to myself, trying to find some comfort.

Somewhat paralyzed and exhausted from all the events of the night, I looked up at the darkened sky with the stars barely peeking through the smog of the city when suddenly, a noise came from the dumpster. "Give me zat book!" a terrifying deep voice demanded as a head emerged from inside the trash can.

Adrenaline exploded through my weary body and I ran as quickly as I could, holding the book like it was a football. Before I knew it, the stranger leapt out of the dumpster and raced after me. The notes in the back of the binding were loosely flapping as I struggled to keep them tucked in. Suddenly one of Dr. Wright's notes fell loose to the ground. I stopped to go back and retrieve it when I saw the mysterious man rounding the corner and gaining on me. Seeing his unruly determination, I left the page on the ground and continued my frantic pursuit for the front of the hotel. I glanced back to see him pick up the fallen page. It seemed to pacify him, because once he retrieved it, he stopped chasing me.

I entered the hotel out of breath and probably looked like I just saw a ghost. "Everything all right, Mr. Blackwell?" inquired the bell captain.

"Oh yeah, everything's good. Just out on a nightly run," I

replied, gasping for air.

"You like to read while you run?" the captain continued with one eyebrow raised, and glancing at the book in my hands.

"Haven't you ever heard of speed reading?" I joked as I walked past the very inquisitive bell captain. He chuckled then returned to his nightly duties.

Finally, I was back in my hotel suite exhausted, yet wide awake wondering who in the world was chasing me tonight. How did they know I had this book, and why would they want it? An unsettled feeling came over me as I played out the possible conclusions to my questions. Someone else must know about the basement, and what was down there.

I looked at my watch, "1:30 a.m." I whispered. It was too late to call Kimberly, so I just sent her a text message. "Sorry I didn't call. Talk to you in the morning. Love you!"

My mind still racing, I removed Maxwell Wright's notes from the back of the leather binding and spread them out on the table. I noticed they had numbers in the bottom left corner, so I organized them by page number. There was a total of eight pages, but there should have been nine. I had all the pages lined up one through eight with no gaps, so I assumed page 9 was in the hands of whoever was chasing me tonight. I finally began to relax as I laid down and read the top of page 1: "The observation of people's language."

Chapter 4

The Observation of People's Language

The next morning I awoke wondering if the entire night had been a dream. However, as I glanced at the night stand and saw the unwritten book with the notes spread on the table, I became conscious of how real it was. Was Clem serious when he said to meet him in the hotel attic this morning?

Just then my hotel room phone rang. I was relieved to hear Clem's voice. "Did you sleep well?"

"So-so" I replied. "I was just reviewing the notes from your grandfather."

"Oh, have you read page 9 yet?"

Goosebumps engulfed my skin, and I fell silent. Why did he immediately ask about page 9? "Thomas, are you still there?" Clem asked.

"Actually, Clem, I need to tell you something. After we left the basement last night, a man jumped out from the dumpster and began chasing me as if he knew what I had in my hands. The pages were coming loose and one of them dropped to the ground. The man who was chasing me picked it up and ran off with it."

There was a long pause until Clem finally responded. "What page number did the man get?"

I hesitated, "As far as I can tell it was page 9, as I only have pages 1 through 8. Clem, tell me what was on page 9, and who would have known about the basement and all of this? I thought you said we were the only ones who knew about it."

Another long pause came between us. "Thomas, I am going to have to call you later. Just continue working on the book with the notes you do have."

"Wait Clem—" But before I could get some answers he was gone.

I was troubled by the thought that Clem was so short with me after I told him someone had stolen page 9. Someone else obviously knew we were in that basement. Why was page 9 the first page Clem asked if I had read? With this turmoil and rapid fire language in my head, I realized I was losing control of what I wanted to happen and how I wanted to feel. I began to observe my own language, which seemed to break out of its path like a raging flood. I was in a state of reaction instead of action. I was letting the situation dictate my reactive internal language.

I took a deep breath and said aloud, **"I am in control."** With this real consciousness, the reactive head chatter ceased, and I was able to think clearly again. Although I didn't understand the magnitude of it all, I accepted that "it is what it is, and I have chosen to complete it." There would be no effective productivity if I remained in a state of fear and reaction. This would give up my power making me powerless.

Gradually, a sense of clarity and resolution started coming over me. I no longer would have the luxury of playing small in life. I recognized this would serve no purpose. The fact that Clem and his father had confided in me and had given me the charge knowing I could bring this book to life sparked an untapped belief in me. *If they felt I could do it, then why not believe it myself?* I thought.

With this heavy decisive emotion, I got on my knees and pled with God to help me carry out the mission that lay before me. I stood up, took the empty book, and whether I was ready or not, began to write. Because my doubts and fears were ever present, I noted my thoughts on the matter. A quote I had committed to memory from William Shakespeare seemed to resonate:

"Our doubts are traitors, and make us lose the good we oft might win by fearing to attempt."

I reflected and continued to write. Too often our doubts rule the day; our fears guide us to a point of indecision, and as a result, nothing is accomplished. This was my day of decision to let my faith overrule my doubts and fears. I resolved that doubt and fear would no longer be welcome in my world, and my words needed to be congruent with that fact. I penned another quote that came to mind from the late philosopher George Addair who summed it up perhaps the best:

"Everything you've ever wanted is on the other side of fear."

I couldn't help but question, "Why was I the one to write this book?" As my internal questions surfaced, consoling reassurances seemed to respond. I had observed people's communication for many years, and the patterns of success therein. I have read, studied, and applied the words and actions of those who have achieved great things. I've long treasured up the wisdom imparted to me through their writings and sayings.

The words of Ralph Waldo Emerson remind me that,

"When a decision is made, the universe conspires to make it happen."

I made a decision last night to be the one to write this book and now it was time to trust the process. It made more sense now that Emerson also said:

"Self-trust is the first secret of success."

Throughout the years that I have been in the business world, I have noticed that many don't achieve their desired results because they have just not decided yet! A thought came to me pertaining to our language and decisions, so I took the book and noted:

Once a decision is made, one must speak it into existence.

My confidence was progressively building, so I looked at page one of Dr. Maxwell Wright's notes.

The Observation of People's Language

Listen to how we greet each other; pay attention to see if people are verbalizing what they want or what they don't want. Are people generally positive or negative? Is there a disconnect between their language and their commitments? Are there any 'disclaimers' in their language? When people talk do you believe what they are saying? Observe people's language then evaluate the lessons learned.

Only say the things you actually want to happen…we bring about what we talk about.

Needing a breath of fresh air, I wandered out to the balcony of the hotel suite with the mostly empty book and a pen, taking in the morning sun as it crept up the Boston skyline. It was still early before the city awoke with its commercial interests. I took in a deep breath, and as I exhaled I allowed my mind to clear and take in all that this glorious day would bring. Thinking on what Dr. Wright wrote on page 1, I realized I had to first become a prime example. With a determined resolve, I consciously committed my thoughts and words to only positivity and creation of the things I actually wanted to happen.

I visualized myself observing other people's language as I sat on the pristine balcony and what that might sound like. Just then, my mind recalled when I was in an exclusive audience listening to the incredible Jack Canfield. I felt it was applicable, so I began to write.

Jack described what a game-changing formula was for me.

E+R=O (Event + Response = Outcome).

Regardless of what occurs in our lives, how we respond determines the outcome. Our response is the one thing we have total control of, but how many of us respond out of control?

Wouldn't it make sense to start our days with positive words that would facilitate positive outcomes, before the event occurred? A daily affirmation, or pre-response (before the event), I have long since adopted is: **"My life is better than expected, and my expectations are pretty high!"**

I closed the book and felt energetic, and ready to facilitate the day. I quickly showered and got ready to get out and observe the language of others. I was at the door of my hotel room, ready to leave, when the distinct thought halted me. "Remember Him." I recognized the source of the thought and said, "Forgive me" as if I was apologizing to someone physically in my room. I went to the side of the couch, dropped to my knees, and prayed in gratitude for the many blessings that were mine. Before getting up, my mind was fixed on the end table drawer. I opened it hoping to find what I was looking for. Sure enough there it was—the best-selling book of all time. I took the book in my hands and it fell open to Romans 8. My eyes gravitated to verse 28: "And we know that all things work together for good to them that love God, to them who are the called according to His purpose."

I glanced at the clock; it was 8:30 a.m. After reading that beloved verse in Romans, I decided to call Kimberly before I went out to observe people's language.

{Power Paragraph}

{I confidentially shared some highlights from the night before and the charge I had been given, and I told her I would fill her in with more details when I got home. It was too much to rehearse over the phone. We prayed together over the phone, as a family, as is our tradition whenever I'm away. After the prayer, I shared with those most precious girls my experience of effortlessly opening up to Romans 8:28. This was perfectly aligned, because a couple of years earlier we had decided as a family to make this our family creed. That was then becoming a sacred time, as we were dealing with the loss of our third daughter. We knew we could have taken the low road and cursed the heavens for such a tragedy; instead, we decided to take the high road and believed that all things work together for our good, somehow, some way. We essentially decided to change our language from two words to four words. Instead of saying "Why me?" and wallowing in the state of a victim or powerlessness, we embraced the words **"What can I learn?"** We did this to remain empowered and to receive knowledge and understanding from those trying circumstances. And, it has made all the difference. Since then, our tradition has continued. Every morning after our family prayer we all say together, **"Everything always works out for our good, because we love God."** I even changed my cell phone voicemail greeting to say "Everything always works out for our good." We truly believe this, and I realized we have spoken it into existence in ALL things. That's the promise.}

Before hanging up, we expressed tender good-byes, and I told Kimberly I was planning on catching a flight home tomorrow. I needed one additional day to observe people's language and connect once more with Clem. I carefully took Dr. Wright's notes and counted them to make sure I still had eight pages. I put the notes in the hotel room safe and locked them in, not wanting to take any chances.

While going down the elevator, I stopped at the third floor so a young couple could come on board. I was alone to that point, and this would be my first interaction with others for the purpose of observing their language. "How are you both this morning?" I said gleefully as I broke the uncomfortable silence of many elevator rides.

"Not too bad," said the young man, likely in his mid-twenties.

"Pretty good," followed the young woman. They didn't ask how I was doing.

"Big exciting plans today?" I urged them along, attempting to get more dialogue from them.

They looked at each other and a silent conversation ensued between them that I seemed to hear loud and clear. *Do you want to tell him, or should I tell him? I'm not sure what the big plans are; are they exciting? This is a lot of effort to talk to people in the elevator.* Then she sternly smiled at him letting him know that it was his lot to answer.

"We'll see," was what the young man came up with. The elevator doors opened suddenly and the young couple hurriedly made their escape.

The doors closed and I was again, alone in the elevator, so I pushed the top floor and decided to take the trip again. This time on my way down a woman with a name badge attached to a lanyard around her neck entered the elevator. It appeared to be a badge that one would receive while attending a conference.

"Hello, Amber. Heading to a conference today?" She looked at me strangely and wondered how I knew her name. Then it dawned on her that she was wearing the name badge as she looked down, then laughed, somewhat easing the tension. She was definitely in a lighter mood than the younger couple, so I was hopeful that her communication was going to be more uplifting.

"Yes, I have a conference all day today. They are always long and exhausting!" she stated with confidence, as if that was the only possibility.

"Always?" I challenged with a soft tone.

"Unfortunately, yes. Always!" she confirmed. When the sliding metal door opened, I was at a loss for words.

Did I say, "Have a great day" or just say "bye, Amber"?

Then, not wanting to succumb to her negative outlook, I blurted, "Have the best day, Amber. I hope this conference is surprisingly intriguing and exhilarating for you."

She began walking away but acknowledged what I said by throwing her head back in my direction while saying, "Hah! We'll see."

Recognizing the elevator to be a powerful resource for observing the language of others, I decided to ride to the top floor once again. Just before the door closed on the ground floor, I noticed a figure rushing toward the closing elevator door, a treacherous apparatus that is no respecter of persons. I hurriedly pressed the "open door" button on the control panel. The nearly-shut door popped open revealing a clean-cut man in a grey pin striped suit, perhaps in his mid-fifties. Positive energy spilled out from his being as a picturesque example of a successful person. There was a pleasant aftershave aroma that accompanied him that prompted me to think, *He even smells successful.*

"Thank you kindly young man," he said with a soothing voice as he strolled into that fancy box that takes us to new heights.

"What floor can I select for you sir?" I managed to say without being overwhelmed with his presence.

"If we're going up, we might as well take this thing to the top," he said with a confidence and tone that gave me a sense that going to the top of his endeavors, whatever those might be, was commonplace for him. "I really do appreciate you opening that door for me. I have a meeting on the top floor that I am going to be on time for," the man continued.

"Of course, you would have done the same kind gesture

for me," I replied.

"Yes I would young man. Yes, I would. That's why **great things like that are always happening to guys like us,"** he concluded.

Recognizing his last words as some I had previously adopted into my vocabulary, and hence my life, I quickly responded, "Yes they are, my friend, yes they are!"

Suddenly the elevator bell rang, indicating we were at the top floor. As the door opened, everything in me wanted to follow this gentleman and continue the conversation that instantly lifted my emotional state to the highest level. The elevating words came easily to me as I bid him farewell, "Have the best meeting today!"

He turned and looked me in the eyes and said, "You can count on it my friend." He briskly glided down the hall to his meeting that was going to be a sure victory. How would I know that without being present in the meeting? Because he said so, of course!

I stood there in the hallway of the top floor somewhat mesmerized by the contrast among the three different encounters I'd had. I needed to find a spot to sit and debrief my observations on paper. As I glanced down the hall in the opposite direction a man stood there, reading a magazine. Was he locked out of his room, and why was he just standing in the hallway? It didn't seem normal, as it appeared he was attempting to cover his face rather than read. I could sense he knew I was looking at him with skepticism. The silence was broken when his cell phone rang, and he began to walk away from me. I couldn't help but notice that he had a thick foreign accent, and as he walked away he looked back at me as if to verify that I was not following him. A disturbing memory flashed back to me as I remembered the shadowy subject who chased me just the night before. This prompted me to quickly make my way back to my hotel suite and check on the notes I had placed in the room safe.

A big wave of relief washed over me as I found the notes securely in their spot. With Dr. Wright's notes in hand, I locked the hotel room door and went over to the desk and began to write my thoughts and conclusions in the book.

Earlier this morning, when I asked the first young couple how they were, his response was, "Not too bad." She followed with, "Pretty good." Next, I inquired if they had big exciting plans today, which after a long pause was met with, "We'll see." The question is, did the young man really mean that he is bad (meaning not good, contrary to the Michael Jackson song) and just not too bad? Did he wake up today saying to himself, "You know, today should not be too bad if I really put my mind to it." Or, was this just an automatic response he has adopted?

The young lady was certainly better than "Not too bad." However, there was a hesitancy in her tone that was echoed in the way she said, "Pretty good." It was well below the level of the standard "good." His retort of "we'll see" when it came to their plans for the day left it totally open to dysfunction or bliss, depending on how the wind was blowing.

As ludicrous as it sounds, people invite what they don't want daily. I know that deep down this couple wants to have an enjoyable day of excitement and goodness, yet their language was nowhere congruent with that outcome. Instead it will be bad for sure, just "not too bad." She will have a marginally better "pretty good" experience. Hmm, I guess "we'll see."

I attempted to write down all the positive things this couple could have said to ensure a more beautiful, pleasant day when I noticed the title of page 2 in Dr. Wright's notes. *"The rate of vibration our daily greetings bring, and how to easily raise them to a higher level."*

"I predict I will be addressing that in the next chapter," I determined. An energizing audible thought came to me, "Everything in its due course, my boy." Perhaps the sensation came from the late Dr. Maxwell Wright himself, speaking from the invisible world beyond where those who pass away dwell. Regardless, I was clear that I alone was not writing this book. Far from it, in fact.

I focused back in and continued to write. Amber, the second gal I met, had a sure confidence about how her day was going to go. Unfortunately, it was not going to be a delightful day as she affirmed, "I have a conference all day today, and they are always long and exhausting!" Even when I challenged the absolute statement, she quickly said, "Yes, always!" There was no way out for Amber. No other option other than long and exhausting. "Why?" you ask, because that is how it "always" goes for her. Raise your hand if you would like to be at dinner with her tonight . . . .

I am actually grateful for Amber's response, because she brings up an important detail. When we use what I call absolutes like *never* and *always*, there can't be any room for flexibility. So, you'd better be sure that it is what you want, because it will be set in stone. Can an absolute be used as a positive? Of course. I use several absolutes every day:

"<u>Everything</u> <u>always</u> <u>works out</u> for my <u>good</u>" and **"<u>Great things</u> are <u>always</u> happening to me!"**

I say them on positive purpose because these are things I absolutely want to happen. I wish I could go back to Amber and simply ask her if a long and exhausting day is what she really wanted. Inevitably she would say, "No, of course not!" The truth is, her conference might very well be long, and she might very well grow tired after such an extensive day. She could recognize that and ease into the optimistic by saying a statement such as, "Although these conferences tend to be long, and I am exhausted by the end, it's worth it because I always come out a better person at the end of the day." Through this method, she could have used the absolute and turned it into something worthwhile. Some additional thoughts came to mind regarding how our words are in charge. I continued to write.

Our mind, body, and universe only know to obey what we command.

The crew always obeys the captain, and we are the captain. There is no internal filter that can make a judgment call like, "Stop, halt, hold on, the captain of this ship just said everything was going to be terrible! Now we know none of us want that, so let's just hijack this vessel and change the course towards the promised land of happiness regardless of the orders she just gave us." Oh, wouldn't that be nice! However, the blessed reality is our body, mind, and environment only know how to respond to our command. In Amber's case, enriching, affirming words to build up her physical strength could be used as well, and she would find that being exhausted doesn't have to attend the conference with her.

I grew increasingly excited as I realized it was time to evaluate the experience I had with the third gentleman in the elevator. He obviously understood, on multiple levels, the essence of the principle that we bring about what we talk about. His demeanor and language were commanding, yet seemed to be humble and approachable. His gratitude for me holding the door, which he expressed twice, lifted my spirits instantaneously. I was intrigued how he declared that he was going to be on time for his meeting instead of succumbing to the phrase, "I'm late for my meeting." The fact is, he probably was in a hurry and perhaps running a little late, but his language over-powered that negative feeling we create when things are not currently how we want them to be. I felt like he knew how to make the best of a situation, and I am clear that this is who he is, because of his daily habits. He's been practicing for a long time as it was totally native to him.

I took confidence and called him "my friend," perhaps because he was so friendly. We even had some things in common when he said, "That's why great things like that are always happening to guys like us!" I had been saying a similar phrase for quite some time, so I felt like we were members in an elite club of sorts. The icing on the cake was when he turned around, despite his obvious need to get a move on, looked me in the eye and genuinely expressed, "You can count on it, my friend." He could have easily brushed me aside, or just responded over his shoulder with a wave, but he didn't. He took the time to align his **body language, tone, and content** at their greatest levels to express those parting words.

I gently put my pen down on the pages of the book, took a deep breath, and began to reflect. As I thought of myself personally, and the history of my responses to people and situations, I admitted that I could relate to all three of the examples at one point or another. I came to grips that this was going to take some **consistent effort. It requires willing conscientiousness and desire** to arrive at the level comparable to the successful gentleman I met today. The sobering realization came over me that I am still "becoming" and have certainly not yet arrived.

I noticed the day was coming to a close as the magnificent ray of light from the sun setting beamed through my top floor hotel suite. I had spent the better part of the day noting my observations in the book. My body felt a little wearied from the late night before, and with some mysterious man lurking about, I did not feel it safe to leave my room—especially at night—so I just ordered room service.

The best part of my day was to hear Kimberly and my sweet girls' voices over the phone. Liberty was making the cutest baby sounds, which yanked on my heart strings. I was definitely excited to get home tomorrow.

I felt it was a successful day of observing the language of others, although there was a lingering feeling of uneasiness due to the fact that I had still not heard from Clem. He left me no way to contact him, and I still had a lot of unanswered questions.

Before retiring, I laid out all the pages on the table in my hotel suite. When I looked at the whole picture of the entire book, the task appeared somewhat daunting. Then I reflected on how beautifully the day unfolded by just focusing on one chapter at a time.

Chapter 5

The Rate of Vibration (R.O.V.) of Our Daily Greetings

The next morning, I was jolted awake at 6:00 a.m. by the hotel room phone ringing. You know, the sound that explodes like the building is on fire? Scrambling to pick it up, I mustered a response that branded me as barely waking up.

"Thomas, I need you to meet me in the lobby before you fly out today," the voice said.

"Clem, is that you?" I hoped.

"Of course it's me, who else . . . anyway, just meet me in the hotel lobby at 8 a.m., and be sure to brush your teeth." He said with a stern yet self-amused tone.

Sixty-seven percent awake, I put my hand in front of my mouth to test my breath. In hindsight, I probably shouldn't have done that, as I knew it was not going to be pleasant. However, on the positive side I felt like I was at least 85 percent awake now. "You see, great things are always happening to me," I mustered with the voice that registers an octave lower in the morning.

Since I had a little bit of time before I headed down to the lobby, I thought it wise to read Dr. Wright's notes on page 2.

The Rate of Vibration Our Daily Greetings Bring, and how to easily raise them to a higher level.

People have adopted a way to respond when greeted by another. Many of our responses have a low vibration that keeps us from operating at a higher level of effectiveness, happiness, and confidence. We can increase our vibration just by simply changing how we greet one another.

I dropped to my knees and thanked the Lord for the insights that were given, and asked that He would give me strength and safety for my journey home. My days always seem to go better when I start and end on my knees.

I sat down and began to write in contemplation of the rate of vibration and the law of vibration. This makes perfect sense, as I already knew and believed what Albert Einstein said when he posited, **"Everything in life is vibration."** Just as a pebble creates vibrations that appear as ripples traveling outward in a body of water, our **thoughts and words create vibrations** that travel outward into the universe, and attract similar vibrations that manifest as circumstances in our lives.

Positive Vibration = Positive Circumstance

Negative Vibration = Negative Circumstance

Many studies have confirmed that everything resonates at some level of vibrational energy. This is also true regarding attitudes and affect. The feelings of fear, grief, sickness, worry, doubt, depression, and despair vibrate at very low frequencies. The feelings of love, joy, abundance, peace, happiness, and gratitude, in contrast, vibrate at much higher vibrational frequencies.

How is it our daily greetings can set the tone of our daily operational vibration? Our vibration responds to our thoughts and words, so when we declare anything that is negative, our state of being responds and operates at that level. The same consequence goes for positive thoughts and words. So when we think about how many times a day we greet another person or even a circumstance (i.e. our responses to events in our lives), shouldn't we be more highly conscious of what we say?

I began to brainstorm and think of the several greetings one might submit to just by being asked, "Hi, how are you?" I decided to put these into categories. It's important to recognize where you are currently, based on your daily greetings. Then you can adopt some salutations that operate at a higher rate of vibration.

Low R.O.V. Responses: Not bad, Not too bad, All right, Can't complain, Hanging in there, Okay, Fine, Still here, Don't ask, Ask me after this week, It's Monday—what do you expect, I could be better, Do you really want to know, You don't want to know, Better than I deserve, I'll be good in about an hour (a popular comeback of employees when it's close to quitting time), and Just another day.

Some of these low R.O.V. responses certainly don't mean that your life is terrible, but could they be better? Remember, everything carries an energy with it, especially what we decide to verbally declare.

{Power Paragraphs for Immediate Implementation}

{High R.O.V. Responses: (For full effect add a double exclamation point {!!} at the end of each greeting) Fantastic, Incredible, Great, Wonderful, Phenomenal, Amazing, Sensational, Marvelous, Outstanding, Remarkable, So Good, Every time I check I am fantastic, Better than expected—and my expectations are pretty high, I feel so blessed, Today is full of miracles, I feel so grateful, I am excited about life, I feel powerful, I am at peace, I am so happy, Two steps above incredible, Today is an extraordinary day, Awesome because everything always works out for my good. I feel good . . . oh, I feel so good, hey! (Use good judgment on that last one). Even Bill Murray, the psychologically challenged character in *What About Bob,* knew the deal when he replied, "Mashed potatoes and gravy, Marie, I couldn't be happier."

Pick some responses from the paragraph above that resonate with you. Then pick one or two that might even be a stretch. Just by expressing these high-level words aloud to yourself you will elevate your own R.O.V. Go ahead, give it a go!}

If you want to get great new results, you have to do great new things.

Just as I finished writing down my thoughts on the rate of vibration in the book, an experience came to my mind.

A few years ago, my father-in-law passed away at the young age of sixty-five. He had battled cancer and Lou Gehrig's disease for many years and finally passed on from this life to the next.

One day shortly after his passing, my mother-in-law called me. She explained that she was doing well, and that knowing that there is a greater eternal plan than just life and death gave her a sense of calm. She felt empowered and *knew* she would see and be with her husband again.

"O death, where is thy sting? O grave, where is thy victory? . . .
But thanks be to God, which giveth us the victory through our
Lord Jesus Christ." 1 Corinthians 15: 55—57

Actually, the reason she was calling revolved around dealing with other people as they greeted her. Their energy was so low and debilitating. When they called her or communicated in passing, they immediately assumed she was depressed and in a very low state. She felt like she was having to lift them, even though she was dealing with her own loss and not theirs. After a typical conversation, she would feel worse than before the conversation. From the moment of their greetings, the conversations would take on a very sad tone. "So, how are you holding up, or how are you getting along?"

She started to feel that maybe she was not supposed to feel at peace. She wondered how she could possibly change this. I asked her, "How do you really feel?"

She quickly retorted, "The fact is **I feel empowered and grateful** for the knowledge of a greater plan."

"Well then. That should be your response." I advised. "This will quickly raise the state (a.k.a. vibration) of the greeter and yourself, and it will do you both a great service by operating at a higher level." I continued. She vowed to give it a try and let me know the outcome. It wasn't very long before I received another call from her letting me know that it absolutely worked! People immediately broke out of their states of depressing assumptions, supposedly on her behalf, and delightful conversations ensued.

We each operate at a level of R.O.V. especially when we are the instigators of our typical everyday greetings. When we are the ones to say, for example, "Hi, how are you?" we can set the tone at a higher level just by adding enthusiasm in our tone and by smiling. This is an immediate game changer! I encourage you to reap the fruits by adding a little more energy (not overbearing) in your salutations—and the smile is crucial. You will see that you too will be lifted instantaneously along with the person you are greeting.

One way to raise another's R.O.V. immediately is to give them a compliment, before you ask how they are doing. This can be done with people you meet for the first time, or someone you know well, such as a friend, family member, or co-worker. For example: "That's a great looking jacket; how are you today?" "Incredible job on that report the other day; how's your day going?" "So happy you could make it to our meeting; how are you?" "Of all the sights I've seen today, you are my favorite; how was your day?"

Crafting that last example caused me to think about the love of my life, Kimberly. I had to catch the mid-morning flight back to Richmond. I was so excited to get home to see her and my sweet girls. I glanced at the clock; it was 7:33 a.m. I jumped from my chair as I realized that I had to meet Clem in the lobby in about thirty minutes and I hadn't even showered yet.

Twenty-five minutes later, it was a solo ride down the elevator to the hotel lobby. I had Dr. Wright's notes secured in the hard leather-bound book. Those blank pages were starting to fill with the chapters of this movement with which I was charged. Just then my cell phone rang with an unfamiliar number. I decided to let it go to voicemail, as I was in a hurry to meet Clem.

Remembering the events from a couple of nights ago when I found the mysterious basement, my mind drifted to the notion that maybe the lobby meant "somewhere else." I was relieved when I found Clem sitting in a corner chair in front of a majestic window that towered over "the yard." The yard used to be the space where the inmates could go outside to catch a breath of fresh air while incarcerated. It was now a courtyard for gatherings and was the spot I escaped to the other night following the contest when I read the letter written by Clem's father.

Clem was engaged in a conversation on his cell phone when he noticed me. He quickly held up his index finger, the universal sign of, "Give me a minute, and I'll be right with you." I couldn't help but observe that after Clem was aware that I was near, he strategically turned his head to the side and lowered his voice. It appeared he did not want me to know what the conversation was about or with whom he was speaking. Suddenly he faced me, still on the phone, and with an audible voice said, "I got it, thanks." The conversation ended and he motioned for me to come over.

"Thomas, how are you this morning?" Clem greeted with his hand extended to me. "I see you have the book and the notes," as he pointed to the contents of my right hand.

"Today is full of miracles, and I am so grateful! How is your incredible morning going?" I answered with belief and a smile.

"Well, not too bad, I guess; still here," Clem mustered. He obviously needed to read Chapter 5 to level up his daily greetings. "Come sit down, Thomas, I need to explain a few more things," Clem started.

Many thoughts raced through my mind as I attempted to resolve the unanswered pieces of who might be forcefully after the information I held in my hand. And who else knew about the basement/escape route at the hotel? Just then Clem interrupted my internal conversation. "Do you have the letter you were given after you won the speech contest?"

"Of course," I said as I lifted the front page of the book where the pages met the hard leather binding, revealing the letter. Not knowing if it was a good idea to pull it out, I quickly closed the book cover on it.

"It's okay, Thomas, you can pull it out," Clem said as he scanned our surroundings to make sure no one was near. This time I noticed the envelope in more detail. It was a hotel-branded envelope, and the letter was written in a familiar cursive on the hotel stationery and letterhead. It was folded with precision to fit the envelope with exactness.

"Read the letter again, if you would, please," Clem politely asked. So, I began to read in a hushed tone:

"Dear Thomas, Congratulations on your recent victory. An executive suite has been reserved for you at this hotel for as many nights as you desire. Furthermore, a very important meeting has been arranged for you to meet someone who will help you with your chance to change the world. Tonight at 11:00 p.m. sharp, you are to report in the basement of the hotel for further instructions. Again, we congratulate you."

"I imagine you are wondering what that really means when it says your chance to change the world, right?" Clem asked.

"Among other things, yes that has been on my mind," I said.

"Here is the plan. You will have one year to complete the book, *The Liberty of Our Language Revealed,* and during that time you will also have several opportunities to speak to various groups. Additionally, it will be arranged that you will have the opportunity to meet many key individuals who will contribute to this movement. In one year's time, we will meet back here at this hotel so you can report on your progress and present the finished book. You are not to share this confidential knowledge about the basement or my grandfather's notes with anyone except your wife. You can, however, share with others that you are writing the book. Do you have any questions?"

"Yeah, about that basement and that scary individual chasing me after our meeting there. I thought you said no one else knew—" I attempted to express my concerns, but Clem cut in before I could finish.

"I am not at liberty to explain all of that right now"—Clem winced at the unintended pun—"as there are certainly missing pieces that I myself am still finding out. I am sorry that happened, and all I can say is you must guard that book with your life."

"Clem, what was on page 9, and why was that the first page you asked if I had read?" The tone of my question left no escape. Clem sat back in the lounge chair, folded his arms, and took in a deep breath, contemplating how he would respond.

"You see, Thomas, in many cases I am just the messenger. Yes, I have a lot of insight, but I don't know everything that is written in my grandfather's notes. As it was explained to me by my father, page 9 contains the notes that could ignite another movement in addition to the liberty of our language. I myself have never read it, but was curious to see what it said, and that is why I asked. I do know that everything always works out for our good, and somehow this will play out how it is supposed to. Page 9 just happened to be the one that got taken." Clem stood as he concluded his thoughts.

"Do you always say that?" I questioned.

"Say what?"

"Everything always works out for our good."

"I actually just adopted it after I heard it on your voicemail," he praised.

"Oh, are you the one who called me a little bit ago?"

"It was indeed, and I'm glad you didn't answer so I could hear your voicemail," Clem confirmed. I was a little relieved that now I had Clem's cell phone number and a way to stay in touch.

"Well, you know where I got it don't you?" I continued.

Clem responded confidently, "Sounds like a Romans 8:28 thing to me."

I smiled and nodded. "That's right, my friend, that's right."

There seemed to be a tighter bond between Clem and me now for some reason. As we bid farewell, he reached out to embrace me with a brotherly hug, which at that point felt comfortable. He told me that he would be in contact to let me know where my next speaking assignment would be, and for now I should get home and keep writing.

The bell captain motioned for an executive car to come over and he requested the driver take me to the Boston airport.

It was the same gentleman who greeted me after I had been chased by the mystery man. On a whim, I asked a bystander to snap a picture of the bell captain and me in front of the hotel entryway. "I'll see you in a year!" I said to the bell captain with no explanation.

Before getting into the car, I took a moment and looked back at the iconic structure. Oh, what a contrast to when I arrived a few days earlier. The whole experience seemed like a dream, or a thrilling movie with an inspirational message tied in. I contemplated that in one year's time I would be returning here to report on a finished book. "It's going to be an exciting and prosperous year!" I said as a farewell to the bell captain.

"It always is, Mr. Blackwell, it always is," he replied with a definitively high R.O.V.

As my chauffeur took me to the airport I opened the book to capture the thoughts that had come to me, spurred on by the response from the bell captain. He seemed to understand the incredible importance of his greetings to the entering or exiting hotel patrons, which set the tone for their experience. This is true of anyone in a customer service role whether it be at a hotel, a grocery store, a retail chain, or any other kind of business. That's why it's so important to hire and train individuals to operate at a high-level R.O.V.

I recalled a study that was done several years ago on the factors associated with the highest successes in the restaurant industry. The researchers looked at key elements such as quality of food, environment, experience, location, customer service, and price. All of these were part of the pie chart, but the two that were the most influential in whether patrons would return to the restaurant were experience and customer service. Kimberly and I certainly proved that early in our marriage when we dove into the restaurant business. Ours was an all-you-can-eat pizza buffet for $2.99. Our product, although good, was not the highest quality per se. Yet, we exceeded previous revenue records and many times had lines out the door. We trained our people to greet with a smile and a cheerful attitude. We put our brightest happiest people at the cash register, which was typically a customer's first point of contact. I got to know people's names and their favorite pizzas, so when they came in I called them by their name and said we'd have their favorite pizza out on the buffet shortly.

I'll always remember one gentleman. I could spot Bob from a distance because his movement was a little slower than others. A stroke caused a severe limp, and he probably should have used a wheelchair as the doctors prescribed. However, Bob wanted to walk, so he muscled through, always with a cane and a smile. He considered every little accomplishment a victory, thus demonstrating he was a winner.

He'd come in at least once a week, and the moment I spotted him at the front door I'd call out loudly, "Hi Bob, I've got your beef and onion coming right up!" Bob loved beef and onion pizza, and even though it was a self-serve buffet, I always personally took some slices of his favorite pizza out to his table.

He'd always say, "Oh Tommy, you didn't have to bring that out to me; I could have walked over and gotten it myself." I learned it was his way of saying, "Thank you, I appreciate your kind gesture to me."

It was the little things, like serving Bob, that made the restaurant business worth showing up for. I also learned that the little personal positive attention that my employees and I gave to our patrons is what kept them coming back.

The deeper lesson is this: We all want to be in an environment where we feel special and respected and where people know our name. The theme song from an old hit TV series, *Cheers,* perhaps sums it up the best: "Sometimes you want to go where everybody knows your name, and they're always glad you came."

The day came when Bob's wife made a special trip to the pizza restaurant by herself. Bob had passed on. She invited me to his funeral, telling me that he would have wanted me to be there as he had considered me a friend. I did attend his funeral, and I was grateful for the friendship that had formed between us, all because of a little expressed kindness and "Bob's beef and onion."

All this talk of onions caused a little moisture in my eyes, and I hung my head a little hoping the driver didn't notice. I summarized my thoughts to wrap up the chapter on "The Rate of Vibration our Daily Greetings."

When we greet people with kindness, genuine interest, and love, inevitably ALL rates of vibration involved will be raised to a higher level. This opens the flood gates for the feelings of joy, abundance, love, peace, happiness, and gratitude. Now comes the time to put this into action.

Remember, knowledge without application remains dormant like a stagnant swamp. When applied, knowledge releases unstoppable possibilities like a commanding river.

Decide and write down five <u>new high R.O.V. greetings</u> you are going to implement today!

1. _____

_____

2. _____

_____

3. _____

_____

4. _____

_____

5. _____

_____

Go to <u>www.saydoachieve.com</u> to receive FREE Weekly Inspirational Language tips.

Chapter 6

The Physical Power of Our Words

I had been only a few days in Boston, yet it felt like months had passed. It was all very thought-provoking how I showed up for the contest and how my language had been peppered with specks of doubt and uncertainty. Now there was a progressive transformation happening in me as I noticed my own language and the R.O.V. with which I greet people.

I was sitting in the coveted middle seat of the airplane when a gentleman sat next to me in the aisle. "Hi there, how are you today?" I beckoned.

"All right," he mustered. "How are you?" he politely asked.

"Life is incredible!" I answered with a smile.

Then something happened that I did not expect. It's as if the higher R.O.V was sort of a shock to his system, because he looked at me like I just said, "I'm from Mars and I just ate a hair brush!" In other words . . . actually there are no other words. You know exactly the look I'm talking about. With such a look I felt he was questioning if I was allowed to think that life was incredible, or if it was legal to be so happy with a long flight ahead while relegated to the middle seat on an airplane. I smiled at the notion and affirmed in my mind, *middle seat or not, long flight or short flight, any which way, life is incredible!*

Cautious of my surroundings, I pulled out Dr. Wright's notes and studied what he had written on page 3.

The Physical Power of Our Words

Our words have the capability to command our environment, including our physical bodies. Our human body only knows to respond to the way we tell it to respond. This also holds true with ALL elements of life on earth; human beings, animals, plants, and especially water.

I pulled out my laptop and connected to the inflight internet. "Why would Dr. Wright include '*especially* water'?" I whispered softly under my breath. Some time ago, I read some material about water and words by a Japanese researcher. I wanted to find out his name and review his findings. I found what I was looking for. Dr. Masaru Emoto was the gentlemen who conducted extensive studies on the patterns of freezing water crystals when certain words were spoken; various genres of music were played; prayers were offered; and water was extracted from a pure, flowing source versus a polluted, stagnant source. I was enthralled as I looked again at the images that were produced. The remarkable difference in the crystal images between *evil* and *peace*, *disgust* and *love and gratitude*, and *you fool* and *thank you* was enough to make the hair stand up on the back of your neck.

http://www.masaru-emoto.net/english/water-crystal.html

I began to write. Could it really be proven that the very elements around us and within us respond with a physical reaction to the words we speak? To the music we listen to on purpose or incidentally? To the prayers that are offered, whether near or far? "This just got bigger than I imagined," I randomly quipped to the gentlemen sitting next to me on the plane who was no longer awake at that point. I determined to do a homemade study of water and words with my family when I returned home.

I closed the book as my mind was now consumed with the excitement of getting home to the most precious people in my life. I briskly walked off the airplane and through the terminal with a self-regarding hope that the loves of my life would be waiting in the receiving area of the airport. A rush of emotion came over me as I spotted them and a homemade sign that simply read, "Welcome Home, Daddy!" Makayla and Charity ran to me for a big welcome-home hug while Kimberly stood back cuddling our little Liberty. I was holding it together pretty well until I caught a clear view of Kimberly's face, which was graced with tears. I held her in my arms, squeezing Liberty May in between, and had a tender moment. By the way we were embracing one another, I'm sure bystanders were thinking I just returned home from a long trip. In all actuality, it was only four days, but there so much had changed since they dropped me off at the airport four days before. The gratitude and emotions of it all came to a head, and when that happens, you can expect some tears from this guy.

The air seemed clearer and lighter as now I had a specific purpose to accomplish. After our girls had gone to bed and Kimberly and I were alone, I related everything that had taken place at the hotel: The anticipation and anxiety of waiting for the judges to determine the winner, the peculiar interaction in the men's restroom, the letter that instructed me to meet in the basement, the check for ten thousand dollars, being led to the basement by a higher power, meeting with Clem in the mysterious basement, the history of the escape route and Dr. Maxwell Wright's story and incarceration, the charge I was given to write the book within the next twelve months, and the creepy man who jumped out of the dumpster and ran after me, making off with page 9. I told Kimberly that Clem would be giving me speaking assignments and certain people to meet to help finish the book. As I recounted all that had happened, I considered the extraordinary responsibility of it all. It was a lot to digest, for both of us.

Kimberly had remained quiet during my extensive explanation. "So what do you think of all of it?" I asked solicitously.

She responded with those same comforting high-level words she had bid me just a few days before: "I believe in you." "I know you can do it, and you have my support," she continued. Kimberly has always believed in me, and has been my number-one cheerleader—even though I am sure that throughout our marriage I have given her plenty of things not to cheer about.

I shall always be infinitely grateful to the Lord for leading me to Kimberly—my best friend and the one I get to spend forever with. We were high school sweethearts, and I knew she was a precious gem the moment I first held her hand. To this day, we can spend the entire day and night together, side by side, and never grow weary of one another's companionship. We can just sit on the couch, hold hands, and words don't even have to be spoken. We dance in the kitchen, even when there's no music. We can't hardly pass each other in the hall without an embrace that usually distracts us from whatever we were doing.

She does so much to make our house a haven of peace and love. She is the ultimate homemaker and unconditional loving teacher to our children. I must have done something right in heaven to deserve her.

The next morning, I was eager to do an experiment with the effects of words on water. I summoned my two oldest girls, eight-year-old Makayla and six-year-old Charity, to help me. This would be part of their homeschooling lesson today. I took two jars and filled them up with tap water.

Then I explained to the girls that there are words that are not appropriate to say in our home and that are damaging to the speaker and those around them when spoken. I referred to them as devilish words, meaning they have no intention of doing us any good—just as the devil seeks only for our unhappiness and destruction. I had them write some of these words on a piece of paper. They wrote things like *ugly, stupid, shut up, you can't do it, iniquity, despair, jealousy,* and *I hate you.*

Then I had them actually say the words they had written to the water. They hesitated, as these were words that had never before come out of their mouths. For the sake of the experiment, I gave them the green light to go ahead and say them. So they went for it, unleashing the venomous words upon the innocent water in the jar. Their faces naturally bore expressions that would indicate that they were not happy—instead, they were in a rage of hate and despair. It's interesting that I did not tell them to make those faces and didn't even recognize they were doing so until I looked at the picture I snapped. We then affixed the negative words to the outside of the jar with tape, sealed it with a lid, and set it aside.

Two glasses of water

The negative devilish words

My girls saying the devilish words to the water

With the next jar, we took a piece of paper and wrote positive words, or heavenly words. These words were in line with the source of all goodness. They included: *I love you, I believe in you, you can do it, hope, you're awesome, beautiful, divine nature, pretty, faith, you are a champion, powerful,* and *confident.* My girls even took it a step further and started drawing hearts, stars, and little figures of our family with big smiles on their faces.

As they had done with the other jar, I then had them say the words to the jar of water. I noticed this time that their faces were pleasant and peaceful. I also became aware that Makayla had one hand on her Bible and the other hand was touching the glass of water. I didn't tell her to do this, but maybe it seemed like a natural gesture to connect those exalted words with the word of God. The good words were then taped to that jar, and like the first, it was sealed.

The positive and heavenly words

My girls saying the heavenly words to the water

I placed the two jars in the freezer and separated them by two pieces of Atlantic salmon (which, had nothing to do with the project). I told Makayla and Charity that we would leave the jars of water overnight to freeze and in the morning, we would see what happens.

I don't think we could have guessed the sight we saw in the freezer the next morning. For one, there was broken glass all over. It appeared that the jar holding the devilish words had exploded, and the frozen water was completely cracked, disfigured, ugly, and almost appeared to be in despair—just like my girls told it to be. On the other hand, the jar holding the heavenly words had stayed mostly intact. There was a little cracking due to the expansion of the water, but the frozen water had solidified into a beautiful, almost divine, and powerful swirl through the center of the block of ice—just like my girls told it to be.

The two jars in the freezer

The negative, cracked block of ice

The positive ice with a beautiful swirl

We were astonished at the results and how these elements took on the physical characteristics of the words that had been spoken. I took out the book and began to write.

The negative water truly was ugly and in despair, and the heavenly water truly was beautiful and lovely. I wanted to continue the experiment with my girls, so I asked them, "How much water do you think our bodies have inside of them?"

"I don't know," Makayla said.

Charity, being the one to more likely take a stab at things, whether right or wrong asked, "A lot?"

I smiled at their individual personalities and said, "The fact is, girls, I don't know myself, so how about we find out?"

We made our way over to the computer and began to look at the different studies on the percentage of water in the human body. The congruent conclusion among the several studies indicated that our bodies hold between 50 and 75 percent water. A new born baby is made up of 75 to 78 percent water, whereas the average adult human body consists of 50 to 65 percent water. The average adult male holds more water at 65 percent; the average female holds only 55 percent. So Charity's answer of "a lot" was pretty accurate. As we read on, we found it interesting how all of our organs depend on water to function. When an individual is overweight, their body holds much less water, which hinders organ function at its optimal capacity.

We took in more from the medical research and were intrigued to learn that water is the primary building block of our cells. It acts as an insulator, regulating internal body temperature. Water is needed to metabolize proteins and carbohydrates used as food. It is the primary component of saliva, used to digest carbohydrates and aid in swallowing food.

It lubricates our joints to enable our movement. Water insulates the brain, spinal cord, and organs, acting as a shock absorber. Water is also used to flush waste and toxins from the body via sweat and urine.

I wanted to draw some conclusions from our water experiment discoveries with Makayla and Charity, so I proceeded with an explanation.

"There is a common phrase, girls, that says **water is life,** and now we can see why. It is literally one of the most important key elements we need to function as humans. What did you notice from the two blocks of ice?"

Makayla chimed in, "It was a little crazy that one was so cracked and ugly and the other one was so beautiful."

Not wanting to be left out Charity retorted with the first thing that came to her mind: "Yeah, I'm never going to say those devil words because I don't want to explode!"

We all had a hardy laugh at Charity's response, and the fact is they both had evidence for their conclusions. We discussed further why it would be so important to **use only words that would cause positive, uplifting, beautiful results**, and how those negative words should no longer have a place in our vocabulary for any reason. As thoughts began to flood my mind I began to write.

The water inside our bodies is the largest force enhancing our health and wellness. Like fresh motor oil is to a well-maintained vehicle, fresh water serves as one of the primary elements in a well-maintained and healthy body. Yet, just because we have plenty of water flowing within us doesn't mean all is well. Our words (positive or negative) set the tone, which directly affects the level of our functionality, whether they be weak or strong, happy or sad, pretty or ugly, confident or doubtful/worried. Then why would any of us say anything that would knowingly cause internal dysfunction?

Another thought on health came to me as I compared motor oil in a car to water in our bodies, so I began to write it down.

I don't believe anyone would consciously pour a bottle of laundry detergent into their car in the place of oil, hoping that just because it has a similar consistency, it will perform the same function. We wouldn't empty a can of soda into the gas tank and expect it to be a valid substitute for gasoline, would we? Of course not! Similarly, how is it that we, as humans, put so many other liquids (besides water) into our bodies and expect an optimal outcome?

I'm not referring to liquids that contain valuable fruits, vegetables, and vitamins. I'm talking about the other stuff that contains chemicals, that when placed directly in contact with a human organ, begin to deteriorate the tissue and hinder the natural function of that organ. I don't feel I need to go through a list of things we should drink and what we should not drink; that's our individual choice. We can, however, make a more powerful choice by asking ourselves before we consume anything, **"Will this contribute to my health or deteriorate it?"**

Likewise, the same evaluation should be taken when we are deciding what words should come out of our mouths: **"Will this bring the results I actually want or bring negative results I do not want?"**

{Power Paragraph}

{The key is being consciously aware. We are the captains of our human ships; nothing comes aboard or gets fired off without our approval. If the captain loses control of what enters or is discharged from his/her vessel, total chaos occurs. Here is an immediate simple course of action to maintain control. Daily, tell yourself (aloud, for best results), **"I am conscious of what I put in my body and very aware of the words that I use."** One idea to help you keep this mindset is to write this affirmation down on a sticky note and stick it to your bathroom mirror. Or my method is to print it, laminate it, and hang it in my shower.}

Makayla and Charity went upstairs to continue their schoolwork, and I got in the zone and was writing. I wanted to show them some of the pictures from Masaru Emoto's water crystal study that I had seen on my plane flight home. Specifically, I wanted the girls to see the water crystals that were captured before and after a prayer ceremony done at Lake Biwa in Japan.

I called them down and we logged on to our family desktop computer. I navigated to Dr. Emoto's website and pulled up the amazing images. I pointed out, "Girls, look at how the lake water is dysfunctional and not pleasant to look at before the prayer. Wow! Now look at that beautiful crystal formation after the prayer!"

"It looks like elegant diamonds," commented Makayla.

"It's a good thing we say a prayer and a blessing before we eat our food," Charity pointed out.

"Yeah, so it doesn't explode," Makayla jumped in with her quick and subtle wit.

Wanting to drive the point home, I soberly commented, "This sheds new light on why it is important to give thanks and bless the food we eat and the water we drink. Wouldn't you agree?" They got the point and we were all even more grateful for our consistent tradition of offering prayers throughout the day and blessing the food we are given.

Just then my phone began to buzz on the kitchen table, so I told the girls they could go back upstairs. It was Clem. I took a deep breath and answered.

"Hi Clem, how is your amazing day going?"

"Love that, Thomas—so blessed, so blessed. And how's the Blackwell family?"

"Life is incredible over here!" I said convincingly.

"Great to hear. Listen, Thomas, you have a speaking request. It's going to be at the Arizona State governor's building to a group of high schoolers who are all leaders at their respective schools. There will be about three hundred students in attendance. These are student body presidents, vice presidents, and such that are coming for a leadership conference. You will be the keynote speaker."

"Wow! That sounds like a great opportunity; thank you," I humbly responded.

"Of course. I'm excited for you to get this message out into the world. I'll make the travel arrangements and send over the details," Clem concluded.

"Here we go, it's all coming together beautifully," I declared to myself while looking at the lovely swirled ice block.

Several weeks later I found myself back in Arizona, where I was born and raised, sitting on the stand of the state representative's assembly hall. My name and bio were read as I was announced as the keynote speaker. I have made it a habit to pray fervently before I speak, right up until the time the first words come out of my mouth. What am I praying for, one might ask? I've learned, the hard way actually, to always give the glory and credit to God for opportunities to speak and to give thanks for anything brilliant that might cross my lips. I also thank the Lord for the chance to be an instrument in His hands, that I might bring an inspirational message to those in attendance. I call this showing up with **humble confidence.**

{Speech given to 300 Student Leaders at the AZ Governor's Office}

After acknowledging those that allowed me to come and speak, and congratulating the students for being there, I got right into it:

"Does anyone have a birthday today?"

(No hands were raised.)

"What about a birthday this week?"

(Still no hands.)

"Okay does anyone have a birthday this year?"

(A ripple of laughter went through the audience as most the hands went up.)

"Okay, I noticed some of you didn't raise your hands which is quite mysterious to me. Surely someone has a birthday this month."

(I spotted a young high schooler who raised her hand. I asked her to join me on stage.)

"What is your name, young lady?"

"Jessica," she said reluctantly.

"Okay, everyone we are going to sing 'Happy Birthday' to Jessica the best we know how!"

(I motioned to the audience and we sang the familiar tune.)

"Now, Jessica, I have a question for you. Do you feel that was the best happy birthday singing this group could have done?" I probed.

"No, I think they can do better!" she contested confidently.

"Okay, let me ask all of you in the audience, do you feel that was your best happy birthday singing?"

(A loud unanimous "no" rippled from the crowd indicating they had more to offer.)

"All right, then, let's do it again. We need to get this right!" I expressed as I gleefully cheered them on.

(Once again, we were singing to Jessica, but this time the volume was a little louder, there was more energy, and a few people used hand motions in addition to their singing.)

(After the second time, I turned to Jessica again.)

"Now, Jessica, was that the absolute very best happy birthday these fellow student leaders could have sung to you?"

(She paused and looked out over the audience, attempting to inform her answer. Some in the audience were nodding their heads, indicating "yes," and yet others knew they could do better and were shaking their heads, indicating "no.")

"No, I still think they can do better!" Jessica said with some

additional pizazz.

"Fellow leaders, is this true? Do you feel you can do even better than before?"

(A roar of agreement exploded from the crowd of student leaders.)

(The third round of "Happy Birthday" was off the charts. Some students were standing on their seats while waving their hands, others were harmonizing, and some even came up on stage and gave Jessica a happy birthday hug.)

"Wow! That was amazing!" I congratulated. "But hold on let—me check in with Jessica."

(Energetic laughter burst from the group.)

"Yes, I feel that was their best effort!" she concluded.

"Now let me ask you, the singers: was that your very best?"

(They shouted a hardy "yes" in unison.)

(Jessica went back to her seat as her peers gave her and themselves applause. I let the noise of their after-thoughts linger a moment, allowing the students to debrief on that experience and their performance. Then I called them back to attention.)

"You know I find it interesting that it took us three times to sing to Jessica in our very best rendition of "Happy Birthday." One of the key elements of superior leadership is to give it our best effort the first time. To play full out the first time. To not do a task or assignment knowing it could have been better."

(Heads began to nod and pens began to hit their notebooks with recognition of individual "ah hah" moments. I continued to emphasize the point.)

*"You see, as leaders in your respective schools, you set the tone of quality, you set the bar of excellence, and **I've learned that those who aspire to your stewardships will typically only perform at a percentage of YOUR very best.** So if you want their performance to increase and be great, your personal performance has to increase and be great! "*

(More pens came out and heads went down to write the revealed leadership discovery)

"How many of you would be interested in a method that would instantly increase your performances?"

(A unanimous vote of hands flung in the air.)

*"Okay, good. Looks like I have the right group here. It's really quite simple; all you have to do is **change your language and you will change your results.** In other words, make sure that the words that come out of your mouths are congruent with what you actually want to happen.*

"Let me explain it in this way: you are the captains, and your bodies and environments are the crews, and they only do what you command them to do. So, none of you would wake up as the captain and say, "All right, crew, let's sink this ship!" Yet often times we say things in a subtler way, not realizing that we are actually commanding the ship to sink. For example, have you ever showed up to school on a Monday and commented that you are not happy to be there and can't wait until Friday because then you'll be happy?"

(A few, who were willing to admit it, were nodding.)

"With such a phrase as I hate Mondays, *you will only sink your Monday success ship. This is just an example of how I want you to start being conscious of the words that come out of your mouths. If you want it to be a great Monday then say, 'I love Mondays and I'm excited to see what great things happen today!' Then watch as the internal crew and environment obey to carry out the order.*

"You see our words carry actual physical power. I'll demonstrate this by showing you how words and water relate. You should know that most of our body is made up of water. Studies have shown that 78 percent of an infant's body, 55 percent of a grown woman, and 65 percent of a grown man's body is water. I tell you this because when words are spoken, the water responds.

"Recently I had my two oldest daughters do a science experiment. We took two glasses of water and wanted to see how differently they'd respond based on spoken and written words.

(I projected pictures on the screen, showing the jars of water we froze, and the radical results when positive verses negative words were used. Wanting to take it a step further, I asked for a volunteer to join me on the stage.)

"I need a strong young man for this next demonstration."

(A trickle of uncertain hands were slowly raised as participants were curious of what they were going to have to do.)

"All right, young man in the blue striped shirt, can you please come up here? Let's give him a hand!"

(The audience consented and cheered him on his walk up to the stage.)

"Hi there, and what is your name?"

"Bartell," he responded with a shy voice.

"Okay, Bartell, I first must ask you if you and I have ever met before, or have we ever had any conversations until now?"

"Uh-uh," he answered as he shook his head.

"All right, what I want you to do is hold out your right arm, and I am going to push down on it with some force, and I do not want you to let me push it down."

(I attempted to push his arm down, but was unsuccessful.)

"You can all see that Bartell is a pretty strong guy. Now let's see how Bartell's strength responds when he uses strengthening, powerful words? Bartell, I am again going to attempt to bring down your right arm with my whole hand while you say the words "I can do it!"

(I put a lot of force on his arm and was once again unsuccessful.)

"Wow! I think I could have done a pull-up on your arm. Now let's change it up a little bit. I am going to again try to pull your arm down, but this time I am only going to use two fingers, and you are going to say the powerless words, I can't do it. *Let's see what happens."*

(As soon as Bartell expressed the words that weakened him, I ripped his arm down with two fingers.)

"Go ahead Bartell try it again, say "I can't do it!"

(He attempted it again and was again defeated by my two fingers.)

"Pretty amazing, huh? Let's keep going, Bartell, because it looks like everyone here is enjoying this."

(A playful string of laughter tickled the audience.)

"Now, my friend, how about we use some other positive words to see how your body and environment responds. I am once again going to use my whole hand and attempt to push down your arm while you say the words, I love you. *I'm okay if you pick someone specific out in the audience that you'd like to direct that to.*

(As the words *I love you* came from Bartell's mouth, I could not budge his arm with my whole hand.)

"Wow, Bartell, I could really feel the love on that one. So, tell me what the opposite of love is?"

("Hate!" immediately spewed from the lips of almost everyone in the room.)

"Let's see if you can sustain my two fingers when you use destructive words like hate. *I would please ask that you do not direct this at anyone in particular this time."*

(The student leaders gasped as my two fingers forced Bartell's arm down with ease, when he uttered the devilish word *hate*.)

"C'mon, Bartell, don't let me push your arm down. Say it again!"

(He was even more weak and exposed this time, as the weakness of hate festered throughout his body.)

"All right I think Bartell has had enough. Now let's get some feedback. Bartell, tell us what your experience was when you used the positive words."

In a solemn voice, wondering how it all happened, Bartell simply said, "That was for real, man. I felt strong and unstoppable when I said the positive words, but when I said those negative words . . . man, there was nothing I could do to stop you from pushing my arm down."

(I gazed out at the intrigued audience to see if they were getting it. Then I turned back to Bartell.)

"Would you be willing to let me take this a step further so another lesson can be learned?"

"Sure man, this is for real!" Bartell responded

"For this next illustration, I want you to select another strong young man from the audience; we're going to give you a break. Give Bartell a hand, everyone!"

(Bartell left the stage saying multiple times, "That was for real, man." He quickly identified another prospect who then came up to the stage.)

"Hi friend, what is your name?"

"Francisco," the young man said with no hesitation, including a tone as if to say there's no way you're getting me down!

"All right, Francisco, this time I am not going to have you say anything, but I am still going to attempt to pull down your arm with my whole hand. This time we are going to write down a bunch of positive words, divine words, on a piece of paper."

(I took out a half sheet of paper and asked the audience to blurt out some positive words to write down. The words began to fly: *Happy, love, champion, beautiful, great, leader, winner, pretty, handsome, incredible. . . .)*

"Okay, that's plenty. Thank you. Francisco, I want you to place this piece of paper with these powerful words written on them against your heart with your left hand. Then hold out your right arm, and let's see if I can push your arm down when these types of words are close to you in your environment."

(I put a significant amount of pressure on his arm knowing he could handle it, but despite my efforts I could not budge his arm.)

"Interesting. You were solid and immovable, Francisco!"

"Okay, everyone, the moment you've all been waiting for. Without swearing you have a green light, for the sake of science, to shout out some negative words, and I am going to write them down. Ready, set, go!"

(The fiery darts began to fly: *Stupid, idiot, loser, ugly, pitiful, hate, liar, fat, nerd, incompetent, gossip. . . .*)

"Whoa, all right! I'm about to fall over up here with all this negativity. I would say thank you, but that would be a little weird for me to be grateful for your weak words. I'm a little concerned that some of you got really excited about that negative part."

(Some laughter broke out—as was my objective to lighten the air a bit after that experience.)

"Okay, Francisco, hold these words against your heart, and let's see if having these words in your environment can affect your strength. Are you ready?"

"Bring it on baby!" Francisco blurted out confidently, insinuating that he was going to be able to withstand the test.

(I raised my two fingers in the air to show the audience that I was not using my whole hand. I looked Francisco in the eye and nodded with no words spoken. His face portrayed a look like when one is about to lift something unusually heavy, and he was fully flexed. Then it happened. With little effort. I pushed Francisco's arm down as though it had no resistance.)

"No way man, try it again!" Francisco shouted, trying to regain his pride in front of his peers.

"Are you sure?" I hesitated.

"Yeah, do it again!" he directed.

"Okay, but just to show you that our words—whether weak or strong—really affect our environment, I'm going to use only one finger."

(He really should have stopped after the first time, because with one finger Francisco was brought down to humility.)

"What do you think Francisco, do written words have the power to strengthen or weaken us?" I asked in a merciful tone.

After a long pause during which Francisco was shaking his head, he humbly replied, "Man, Bartell was right; that was for real."

(A surge of applause and laughter filled the room as Francisco returned to his seat.)

"Let me wrap this up, my young friends. You saw and cannot deny the power of our words. For Bartell and Francisco, they felt it. It's not just about what you say, it's also about the words you hang out with while you're reading, checking your phones, and the text messages you send and

receive. You also saw that when Bartell said hate, *he was the one who was weakened, not the person to whom he might have directed that word. The danger comes when others say destructive words directed at you. Yes they are obviously weakening themselves, but if we decide to believe what they are saying, we take on the weakness as if we had said it to ourselves.*

"My friends, go be leaders from this day forward who are powerful, who are inspiring, and who are excellent at a high level—the first time. Be courageous in eliminating from your lives words that are powerless and devilish, and replace them with powerful and divine language. From this day forward, remember and put into positive action the knowledge you now have that **we bring about what we talk about!**

"May God bless your efforts as you lead and take your respective schools to new levels of greatness. Thank you!"

A thundering, standing ovation erupted, and as I smiled with gratitude I said a silent prayer for these youth that they would be blessed in their efforts to be their best. Afterwards, among others, a young lady approached me who happened to be the student body president of a school in a small town in Arizona.

With tear-stained eyes, she confessed her reason for crying. "Mr. Blackwell, as I was listening to your talk I felt so guilty." Her composure crumbled, and she was now in a full-on cry.

I smiled gently at her and let her regain her ability to speak. "Why is that?" I questioned.

"I feel like I've made my younger sister ugly. I tell her all the time that she's not good enough, and that she's overweight, and that she puts on too much make-up, and . . ."

I put my hand on her right shoulder in an attempt to stop the forceful confession. This certainly stopped the declaration of guilt but spurred on more tears.

"Look at me in the eyes," I said in a consoling voice. "Here's the most beautiful part about all of this: Our intelligent bodies are designed to flush out water and harmful substances daily, including the words and thoughts in our environment. You can immediately apologize to your sister, and moving forward only speak beautiful, uplifting words and all will be made whole."

She smiled. Her shameful tears seemed to turn to gladness as she nodded in agreement and gratitude and turned to walked away.

As the crowd cleared out, I couldn't help but notice that there was a middle-aged gentleman standing in the back who obviously didn't fit the part of a high school youth leader. I was conscious of him taking pictures of me several times during the presentation but didn't think much of it. Now, with most of the audience out of the assembly hall, I glanced in his direction when he subtly picked up his cell phone as if to call someone, and then he was gone.

This prompted me to go to my computer bag and check on the security of the book and Dr. Wright's notes. Something was strange, yet familiar about whoever that was. My mind began to unproductively wander and ask, *Was that the man that chased me at the hotel in Boston? Or, was it the same man I saw on the top floor of the hotel conspicuously reading a magazine while I was observing other people's language?* I ceased such thoughts, as they only brought fear and worry, and I declared to an empty assembly hall, "I don't live in that world!"

Go to <u>www.saydoachieve.com</u> to receive FREE Weekly Inspirational Language tips.

Chapter 7

People Tend to Act How

You Speak to Them

I had a few hours before I had to be at the airport to fly back home to the east coast, so I drove to a familiar place in downtown Mesa, Arizona. When we lived there, this was a place I often went to seek peace and direction. I pulled into the parking lot and gazed at the lush park-like landscape abounding in a myriad of flowers accentuated by shrubbery. I always marveled at the majestic talent and diligence of those gardeners who were somehow able to create a heavenly flower garden in the midst of an oppressive desert climate.

In this contemplative state I felt it was a good time to continue my writing, so I pulled out the book and Dr. Wright's notes. I was ready to move on to page 4, feeling satisfied that I had justly illustrated the physical power of our words from the previous page. I carefully selected page 4 from the notes and began to read.

People Tend to Act based on How You Speak to Them

There is an inborn goodness and nobleness, a drive to be great, embedded in each of us as humans. Our words and conversations directed at others can activate the good in people, OR our words can ignite their negativity or weaknesses depending on how we speak to them. Whatever we are looking for in others (the good or the bad), we will find it, and our words bring to light that which we are looking for. Remember: the key is to see our fellow inhabitants as they can become. Speak to and treat others with kindness and dignity. Let not wrath rule thy tongue, and watch the transformation.

My mind quickly went to our earlier experience in the restaurant business. With this prompting, I started the car and drove to the nearby location on the southwest corner of Gilbert Road and Southern Avenue where the restaurant we managed was located. We had been married less than a year when some friends of ours asked if we would like to get into the restaurant business. I was twenty-one and Kimberly was twenty, and we thought we could do anything, so we agreed.

I arrived at the now vacant building attached to the other businesses in the commercial plaza. I parked in a spot that enabled me to have a clear view through the windows of the once bustling all-you-can-eat pizza buffet.

My surroundings prompted me to take out the book, and I began to write down the memory I felt would help illuminate this area of focus.

The fact is, Kimberly and I didn't know a lot about the pizza buffet business—nor for that matter, the restaurant business—so we relied heavily on the training we received from the family that owned it. Eventually the time came when the management of the pizza operation was to be completely turned over to us. I'll always remember that day. I was sitting in the office with the previous manager and owner, and they imparted one last piece of advice to me.

"You see that gal out there cooking?" one of them asked.

"Yes," I responded.

"Her name is Tonya, and one of the first things you'll probably want to do is go ahead and fire her." No explanation followed.

"Why should I fire Tonya?" I prodded.

The outgoing manager and owner looked at each other as if to decide who should let me in on the inside information about Tonya, who was potentially about to lose her job. Finally the manager broke the silence and fired off his reasoning: "She's got a terrible attitude, and she often shows up late. She never even brushes her hair or puts on any makeup. She takes too many breaks, she never smiles at customers, and she's just—"

"Okay, I got it," I broke in to stop the verbal beat down of Tonya, whom I'd never met. With that, the two men stood up, wished me the best, turned on their heels, and were gone.

As I reflected on the memory, I remembered sitting in the silent office contemplating how I would handle the situation. I had never fired anyone before, or even hired someone for that matter. I had always made it a point to get to know people personally and then create my own verdict about them rather than relying solely on the perspectives of others. I also knew that what others perceive from the outside of a person is often an inaccurate story about who that person really is on the inside. With these grounding considerations, I stood up and walked out of the office to deliver the message to Tonya based on the advice of the previous manager and owner.

Wearing a subtle smile, I walked intently to the area where all the pizza-making magic happened, "Hi there, I'm Thomas, the new guy here. How are you?" I asked with an upbeat tone in my voice.

There was not much of a response from Tonya—just a low, grunted, "Hey."

"You're not going to believe what that previous manager just told me about you!" I continued.

For some reason, my words struck a chord of terror, and her jaw dropped as she began to walk backward. She must have been anticipating that the next words out of my mouth would be that her days as a cook were finished. However, that's not what I had in mind.

"No, no, Tonya, you must have the wrong idea because they said if anyone can run this restaurant it is you! I am so excited, because I don't know much about the pizza business, and I'm going to need all the help I can get. When you take a break—and by the way, you are welcome to take as many as you need—let me know, because I would like to get to know you better. What a blessing to have you here! In fact, I can see you becoming one of my shift managers."

Tonya looked around to see if anyone else was eavesdropping on our conversation. Then, when she felt it was safe, her face lit up with a beautiful smile . . . maybe for the first time in a long time.

"Are you being serious? Me, a shift manager?" she stammered.

"Of course! You've got leadership written all over you, and

you have a beautiful smile," I complimented with a smile of my own, and then walked back into the office.

You know, it's amazing when you speak to people with kindness and praise and get to know their story. Tonya showed up for work early the next day wearing a smile. Her hair was brushed, and she had a little bit of makeup on her face. All of the previous negative descriptions about her turned around completely to be positives. Tonya became my shift manager and was one of our best workers and leaders. She began to befriend the other employees and speak to them with the same kindness and trust that was shown to her.

Like many of us, Tonya had accumulated a few rough layers from experiences throughout her life. These were covering up and decomposing the gem she really was. I learned that, due to some unfortunate circumstances, she had a two-year-old son she had not seen in eighteen months. I learned that at an early age she was resigned to the parental guardianship of an unstable uncle who had regrettably abused her in every sense of the word. Yes, Tonya had reasons *not* to smile, reasons *not* to care whether her hair was neatly brushed, and perhaps some reasons *not* to respect authority, especially when that authority spoke to her in an unbecoming fashion. However, despite all of that, I had more reasons to believe that she was a special, beautiful, and capable individual who was just waiting to be discovered.

The now-empty windows of the former restaurant seemed to come to life again as I thought about the lives that were transformed. Another impression came to me, so I began to write.

{Power Paragraph}

{I believe that from the moment we take our first breath on this blessed earth, we all come with an invisible yet apparent

Superman-like sign on our chests that reads, **"I Am Loved, I Am Divine, and I Am Worthy of Greatness."** With every mortal experience we encounter, from that moment forward, our treasured sign is either brightened with hope and charity or it is dampened, stifled, diminished and covered up. In Tonya's case it was obvious that her figurative "sign" had been thrown to the wolves, scarred, buried under layers of life's sour experiences. When I decided to speak to her with love, kindness, and confidence, it was as if these damaging layers began to fall away, and we could both see her God-given sign again. Once it was visible, we began to **"Shine her sign"** with continued words of acceptance, kind-heartedness, and friendship. It's not that she became someone different; rather, she returned to who she was meant to be. **Thus the significance of treating, speaking to, and seeing people as they were meant to be**, especially after removing all the inhibiting layers. Then, continue endlessly to shine their sign.}

In the Bible, the Savior Jesus Christ who was the ultimate example of treating, speaking to, and seeing people as they were meant to be—said, "A new commandment I give unto you, that ye love one another, as I have loved you, that ye also love one another" (John 13:34).

Another essential point came to my mind, so I continued to write.

Whether it be good or bad, whatever we are looking for in people or situations, we will find it. We tend to find exactly what we are looking for. As my friend David Bayer (one of the best mindset coaches in the world) always says, "Our brain is a goal achieving machine." Whatever the task decided, our brain will look for evidence to support it.

This perspective is a game changer, as we all have opportunities, at a variety of levels, to interact with other humans. It is also key to remember that **whatever we focus on expands**. If we are constantly looking for the good and praising it, we will get a lot more of it. On the other hand, if we are looking for and recognizing the bad in people and situations, unfortunately, less than desirable behaviors and circumstances will persist. **If you go looking for mud, you will rarely escape without getting yourself dirty.**

What if we were to improve on this right now? I mean that from this day forward, we were to look for and recognize only the good? To speak to people only with kindness, respect, and as they were meant to be by shining their "I Am Loved, I Am Divine, and I Am Worthy of Greatness" sign? My well-founded feeling is that both worlds would change for the better, mainly because when we lift others we naturally elevate ourselves to higher ground.

I drew a deep breath, and felt at peace with both the restaurant experience I penned and the points that were made. Next, I asked in a prayerful attitude, "What else could be written to emphasize the points of this chapter?"

A clear memory came to mind of how a destructive attitude was immediately changed because of some peaceful words that were remembered and spoken. I climbed into my rental car and drove about a mile east to the site of the incident. I slowly pulled into the fast food parking lot where five years earlier I had almost faced a physical confrontation. I closed my eyes to picture that night and all that was involved. Then I took out the book and again began to write.

It was very late, and I was making my way home after a long day of appointments. Just a few blocks away, Kimberly and our two young girls were anxiously awaiting my arrival. I was yielding to oncoming traffic so I could make the left turn into my neighborhood, a turn I had made so many times before. Once I was clear to go, I sped across the opposite lane and was startled when I saw a figure of a man crossing the street to the side of me. I was still a safe distance from him, but it caused me to slam on the brakes. I looked over at the gentleman who was dressed in dark colors, making it even more difficult to see him. I acknowledged his presence with an apologetic wave of my hand. Then as I started to drive again, all of a sudden I heard a loud thud against my car. It was so loud that I pulled over to see what had happened.

Did he just do what I think he did? I thought. *"Did he seriously just throw his water bottle against my car as I passed?"* I glanced over at the side of my car against which I had heard the loud impact. Sure enough, not only had he thrown his bottle against my car out of rage, but he had left a sizeable dent.

I looked up and noticed as the man unapologetically picked up his water bottle off the road, glanced at me with a scowl, and kept walking. With compromised emotions, I immediately recalled the softball bat and tennis rackets I had in my trunk. These might come in handy for something other than for what they were designed.

With this irrational thought, I got back in my car, made a quick U-turn, and prepared myself for a possible confrontation. My mind was set on how much repairing this dent was going to cost me and that it was not my fault that I didn't see him crossing the street. After all, it was dark outside, and he was wearing dark clothing! I began to make my case out loud as if arguing before a judge. "He should have been wearing something more visible; didn't he see me wave at him apologetically?" I was fuming, and my mind was racing as I was stuck at a red light waiting until I could catch up to this man who had just walked off as if nothing had happened.

The red light seemed to be taking an abnormally long time to change, and as odd as it sounds, this prolonged delay turned out to be a great blessing. It seemed as though something else was in control of the traffic light that night and was not going to budge until I changed my attitude. I vividly felt the power of two forces battling within me, leading in opposite directions. One was trying to drag me down to revenge and retribution, and the other was yearning to guide me to the higher road, if I was willing to take it, of forgiveness and understanding. Ultimately, I decided to be open to guidance after simply asking myself, *What is the right thing do here?*

Then I experienced a moment of grace. I believe God found a way to change everything from hate and malice to forgiveness and compassion. It's as if my asking what the right thing was to do allowed His Grace to finally enter my heart. I was calming down with every second the light refused to change. That is when I heard a soft, yet clear voice say words that changed everything.

"Have I not destroyed an enemy, when I've made him my friend?" —Abraham Lincoln.

In high school I had an inspired teacher who wrote a powerful quote on the board every week. These quotes interested me, even as a teenager, and I decided to write them down; I even committed many of them to memory. Isn't it interesting that the words at the red light that night, which audibly came to my mind from a Higher Source were the words of a powerful quote by Abraham Lincoln that I had inscribed into my personal treasury so many years ago? "Have I not destroyed an enemy, when I've made him my friend?"

Internally wrestling in my mind about what was right and

wrestling with what my emotions were tempting me to do, I realized I had a choice. I could create a confrontation and bear the consequences, or I could somehow make a friend with the pedestrian who just put a dent in my car. When I heard that powerful phrase come into my mind, I knew what the right choice was, and my destructive attitude began to defuse.

*"But the Comforter, which is the Holy Ghost, whom the Father will send in my name, he shall teach you all things, and **bring all things to your remembrance**" (John 14:26).*

Finally, the light turned green. I proceeded to drive in the gentleman's direction and pulled into a fast food parking lot. He noticed my actions and started walking forcefully towards me. I knew what I had decided to say, and I hoped and prayed it would change this whole situation. Now he was within audible distance, and I too was walking toward him, but not with the same aggressive approach. My right hand was extended toward him and the words came out of my mouth, "I'm so sorry, sir. I did not see you walking, and I imagine how terrifying that must have been."

His demeanor softened, yet his face manifested a look of confusion. My hand was still extended, and he was making no effort to shake it, so I continued. "I sincerely apologize." With this second plea for forgiveness and my hand still offered, he finally reached out his hand to clasp mine. I remained silent to see if he would say anything. He shamefully looked down at the ground and took in a deep breath.

"I'm sorry, too; it's been sort of a rough night for me," he stammered. Then his confession and explanation began. "I don't usually take walks at night, but tonight I had a heated argument with my wife and decided to walk it off. So I guess I took out my anger on you and your car."

I nodded my head to acknowledge his effort to validate his actions. "No worries; better my car than your wife," I said consolingly. I again extended my hand for a parting handshake and said, "I sincerely hope everything works out." With that, my new friend met my hand in the middle and I returned to my car.

"I say unto you, Love your enemies, bless them that curse you, do good to them that hate you, and pray for them which despitefully use you, and persecute you" (Matthew 5:44).

As I drove away, I felt a deep sense of peace and gratitude. That whole situation could have gone a completely different and regrettable direction. While driving calmly into my neighborhood, I reflected on the miracle of it all.

Then suddenly, the adversary decided to take another defying stab at my spirit with this weakening thought: "But what about the dent in your car? That's going to cost a lot of money to fix!"

I wasn't about to let the prince of darkness have any more influence over me, so I repeated the words aloud that had cast him out before: "Have I not destroyed an enemy, when I've made him my friend?"

Staring into that parking lot now, I was again granted the peace I felt that night by making the right choice. While still in the fast food parking lot, I imagined myself having a conversation with that incredibly influential leader who was the author of that statement.

"Mr. Lincoln, the answer is yes to your inspired question, as I am now witness. We do destroy our enemies when we sincerely make them our friends and speak to them as such."

I started the car and began to wind through the old neighborhood where we had lived several years before. I had driven through these streets countless times, even before Kimberly and I were married, because this is the same area she lived in when we were dating in high school. With her on my mind, I reflected on my high school sweetheart's natural gift of speaking to people with kindness and love. I stopped the car right in front of her old house, and began to write a couple of examples that came to mind of how she did this so beautifully.

On one occasion Kimberly and I were at the airport flying to Hawaii and you could say we were running late. We were at the airline counter checking our bags and the gal working said to us, "Just so you are aware, we cannot guarantee your bags will arrive with you at your destination due to the late check-in."

In an over—powering confident tone I immediately responded with, "Yes they will ma'am, everything always works out for us!" Although the statement out of my mouth was certainly true, the arrogant and somewhat demeaning tone did not set well with the airline worker. Her body language gave me the ominous warning of, "Look, buddy, how would you like it if I sent your luggage to a different continent?"

Just then a sweet voice from over my shoulder said, "That is such a beautiful glass flower pinned on your sweater. It looks like someone special gave that to you." The airline worker's countenance immediately changed from disdain to delight as she smiled at my wife and thanked her for such a thoughtful compliment.

"My grandchildren gave it to me, and I wear it every day," she said with loving reflection in her voice.

I immediately felt the shift in attitude from the airline worker because my wife decided to do what she always does by speaking to others with kindness and thoughtful compliments. Then something unexpected happened as the worker said, "Actually, because of your airline status, it looks like we have an upgrade for you to first class, but it looks like there is only one seat, so both of you would not be upgraded."

I was silent contemplating the situation when Kimberly piped in and said, "That would be great; my husband doesn't mind sitting in coach while I sit in first class." I could only chuckle and agreed that my lovely wife had certainly earned the reward of being bumped to first class. Although I was fully willing to let her sit in first class for the six-hour flight, we decided to give the seat to someone else so we could be together, which was more important.

I recalled another occasion where Kimberly demonstrated the power of this principle. One afternoon while living in Tempe, Arizona, I noticed our two young daughters in the back yard being unusually rough with the precious flowers my wife had carefully planted. A little shocked and perturbed that our sweet little girls would do such a thing, I went straight over to Kimberly, who was working in the kitchen, and pointed out their inappropriate behavior. The way she handled this situation was a huge and valuable lesson to me.

She calmly went and opened the back door, made sure both girls were listening, and said, "Girls, remember these flowers took a lot of time to grow for us to enjoy. Be sure to show love and respect when you are playing around them. Show kindness and love when you touch them and look at them."

"Okay, sorry, Mom . . . we will," Makayla responded without hesitation. And that was that. Problem solved.

That whole situation could have gone in a completely different and harmful direction had I gone out and said with an accusatory tone, "Girls, stop hurting those flowers, what's the matter with you!?" Such words bring on anger and blame instead of love and positive action.

{Power Paragraph}

{What is the big lesson here? When in a position to guide others as a parent, manager, coach, leader, **tell them what you want them to do with love and confidence, instead of emphasizing what you don't want them to do out of fear and anger.** The human ear and brain receive literally what is heard, before any interpretation. That's why it is so important to say what we actually want to happen. For example, if one of my children is standing on the table and I want her to get down (because it is dangerous), how would I say that? I could say, "Charity Kristine Blackwell, don't stand on the table. It's dangerous!" In this instance the child heard, "stand on the table" and "dangerous." Often times that little word *don't* is brushed right over and has no meaning. On the other hand, I could say, "Charity, get off the table and play on the ground where you are safe." This way the recipient only hears things I want her to do, such as getting off the table, playing on the ground, and being safe. In addition, our tone of voice plays an enormous part in how the message is received. If a harsh tone is used, it can automatically trigger a defensive attitude, which diminishes productivity and increases resistance. Whereas a calm, collected tone of voice is received with compassion and understanding, and the desired result is much more likely to occur.}

Go to <u>www.saydoachieve.com</u> to receive FREE Weekly Inspirational Language tips.

Chapter 8

The Language of Gratitude, Thankfulness, and Appreciation

I kept the car running to keep the air conditioning flowing while parked out in the blessed heat when I glanced at the clock. "Yikes!" I shouted, realizing I had to make a mad dash for the airport if I wanted to make my flight on time. Just then my phone rang, and I noticed it was Clem calling. Being the responsible driver that I am, I put in my earphones so I could talk while I drove. "Hi, Clem, how incredible are you, my friend?"

"Life is fantastic Thomas!" he quickly responded, then continued with an urgent tone. "Listen, where are you right now?"

"I'm still in Arizona heading to the airport. Why?" I questioned.

"All right, I need to run something by you, but I need you to pull over so I know I have your undivided attention," he summoned.

"I understand, Clem, but I am heading to the airport and if I want to make my flight—"

"Don't worry, you're not getting on that plane tonight," Clem interrupted.

"I'm not?" I curiously asked as I slowed the car and pulled over.

"No, you're not. We've received a request for you to go speak in Tucson, Arizona tomorrow evening to a group of scientists and professors from the University of Arizona. My father has a strong relationship with this group, and while talking to one them yesterday he mentioned you were in Arizona and that you would be happy to speak to them."

"Oh, he did, huh?" I retorted.

"How familiar are you with the university and Tucson?" Clem inquired.

"More familiar than you know. My parents met at that university, my grandfather and aunt and uncle still live there, and I grew up playing on their tennis courts," I said, reminiscing.

"Great, you'll be speaking at seven tomorrow evening at Biosphere 2," he said, trying to end our conversation without any further details.

"Whoa, hold on—Biosphere 2! To a bunch of scientists and professors? Clem, I am not qualified to speak to those folks," I panicked.

There was a pause in our conversation and Clem was silent for a moment. "If you say so, Thomas," he calmly replied letting me resolve my own concerns. "You *are* qualified, or we wouldn't be asking you to do it. However, it doesn't matter what we think, it's whether you say and believe you are qualified," he sternly said, giving me a taste of my own medicine.

I took in a deep breath and realized I still had a lot of work to do to master this whole movement. "You're right, Clem, I am qualified, and I'll do it," I responded with a higher R.O.V. "What am I being asked to speak about?"

"Hmm, that is totally up to you, my friend, but we have the utmost confidence that you'll speak on the exact topic they are needing. All the best, Thomas." Then he hung up and was gone.

I sat there in my rental car listening to the other cars whiz by, doing my best to take it all in. "Biosphere 2 . . . professors . . . scientists! What would they possibly need to hear?" I pondered. Clem sure liked to stir things up on a moment's notice, and I had a feeling there would be another dose in the future.

I called Kimberly and let her know that I would not be home tonight because Clem had called me with another speaking assignment in Tucson. I also thanked her for giving me some great material to write about in the previous chapter. She reminded me that while I was in Tucson I should visit my grandfather who had just turned ninety-six years "young." I asked her to give our girls my love, and I promised that I would be home in a couple of days. I drove the hour and a half to Tucson that night, and checked in to the hotel Clem booked for me close to where I would be speaking.

While driving, I couldn't seem to come up with any ideas

on my own about what to present. I entered my hotel room a little distraught and concerned that the idea had not come yet, so I dropped to me knees and prayed to know what to do. After what seemed like half an hour on my knees, the simple thought came to look at the next page of notes.

I was a little frustrated that I had not thought of this resource before, yet I was grateful for the divine reminder. I went to my bag and pulled out the leather-bound book and Dr. Wright's notes tucked behind it.

Page 5 simply said this:

The Language of Gratitude, Thankfulness, and Appreciation

One of the highest forms of intelligence lies in the individual who understands the infinite power of being in a state of gratitude for all things, both good and challenging. No degree from a university can guarantee that you will achieve it. No amount of money can buy it, and no person can possess it while living in a state of pessimism. I would submit that some of the most influential words in the human language are uttered when one offers a sincere "thank you."

"The most evident token and apparent sign of true wisdom is a constant and unconstrained rejoicing." — Michel de Montaigne

I sat in solace and contemplated what Dr. Maxwell Wright had written. I found it quite remarkable that he would mention words such as *intelligence, degree from a university,* and that thought-provoking quote from Montaigne that revealed a sign of true wisdom. It was all the more remarkable because my very concerns were coming from a vein of how highly intelligent my audience was going to be. Now I felt I had something to offer, and although I wasn't exactly sure on what I was going to speak, I trusted that this was what they needed to hear. "I'm grateful that everything always works out for our good," I mumbled in a drowsy voice.

That night, in my prayer prior to going to bed, I decided to express only the things I was thankful for. I expressed faith and gratitude for what I have and for those things I wanted to occur—not asking for them to occur, rather thanking the Lord as if they had already come to pass. I had done this several times before, but now I really wanted to feel the effects. I noticed how a sense of well-being engulfed me as I prayed and how my thoughts left no room for doubt, worry, or depression. I determined then and there to make this a more regular practice.

I woke up the next morning with gratitude looming large, and I declared it to the world. "Thank you for this beautiful new day!" I used to do this daily when I was serving a religious service mission in South America, but I had fallen out of the habit. I recommitted to implement this life-changing exercise. The key is to express some form of gratitude and positive declaration the moment you wake up. This immediately dispels doom and gloom that might be lurking about competing for your outlook on life that day.

In preparation for my talk, I began to intently study gratitude and its effects on the human experience, both brain and psyche. I also looked into the history of the Biosphere 2 and its purpose.

After studying the subject for a couple of hours, I wanted some fresh air, so I made my way outside the hotel and went for a jog. There was a light rain that day, which I knew did not come all that often to this part of the country. The delicious scent of the water bathing the thirsty, dry desert ground instantly took me back to my childhood. My visits to Tucson had been mainly to visit my grandparents, Grammy and Poppy. Grammy passed away a few years ago, and Poppy now lived in an active retirement facility. My mind began to wander freely on the cherished memories that for me lingered in this place. This city was also where I said my last tender good-byes to their son, my father, who passed away shortly after my seventh birthday. With these remembrances flowing through my mind, I recognized I was putting myself into an elevated state of gratitude. My feet felt lighter as I ran, and a fixed smile seemed to be painted on my face.

Still running and feeling **great-full,** I wondered what would happen to my physical being and stamina if I contemplated life's experiences as being a curse instead of a blessing. Just the thought of it weighed down my feet, and I felt my thoughts going to an unhealthy space. It's as if the moment I let the negativity in, even as an experiment, it tried to break through like a raging river crushes the strongest barriers whenever a weakness is found.

Wanting nothing to do with this negativity, I repeated an unknown author's indisputable poem aloud, one I had long ago put to memory:

All the water in the world,
The highest wave or tide,
Can never sink the smallest ship
Unless it gets inside.

And all the evil in the world,
The blackest kind of sin,
Can never hurt you in the least
Unless you let it in.

Once I was back in my hotel room, I immediately went to the desk and began to write the experiences I had while running. When feeling thankful for life, my state of being was blissful, elevated, and brilliant—I felt like I could run forever. However, when I stepped into the world where the pessimist dwells (even for a moment), my physical body knew no different and began to bog down with buried hopes and misery. Nevertheless, the words of the inspired poem changed the night back to day. Gratitude, thankfulness, and appreciation were definitely the more glorious path to take.

The time arrived for me to speak to the acclaimed group of professors at Biosphere 2. The building illuminated with a mysterious liveliness of wonderment. Hours upon hours of research and development had been dedicated to this project, including a two-year experiment where eight people were challenged to live inside the fascinating structure without any exits. In a nutshell (no pun intended), it demanded an immediate respect for the sciences.

The group was starting to gather in one of their larger meeting rooms, one that held more than two hundred people. Here I thought it was going to be a smaller crowd, but maybe more people had been invited to attend. I made my way to the men's restroom to clear my head and get into the proper frame of mind. Standing at the mirror, I closed my eyes and took in some deep breaths while repeating a few times, "I am so grateful for this opportunity."

At that moment, another man appeared at the sink next to me where he was washing his hands. *Where did he come from?* I thought. I flashed back to meeting Clem in the men's restroom at the hotel where this all started.

"You muscht be zee shpeaker today," the man said with a thick accent. Something about his accent sent a shiver up my spine, yet his tone of voice and energy were very disarming.

"Yes sir, I am the speaker for this evening. My name is Thomas," I said with my hand cordially extended, even though I knew both of us had hands that were still a little wet.

He complied and shook my hand, saying, "Friedrich. It's a pleasure to meet you."

Not wanting to guess wrong, but really wanting to know where Friedrich was from I asked, "I love your accent, where are you from originally?"

"A little town called Kullstedt in Germany. Best vishes on your talk tonight."

In this case I would have guessed right; I thought that was a German accent. I wanted to draw more information out of him, but his back was turned and he was already heading out the door.

"*Danke,*" I said with my best German accent. Friedrich looked back and gave me a slight head nod and subtle smile to acknowledge my attempt to thank him in his native tongue.

My introduction by the host was brief but sincere. He explained that I had agreed to come on a moment's notice, and that his friend (Clem's father) let him know that I was working on a book that was going to generate an influential movement in the world. A refined applause was rendered by the sophisticated audience welcoming me to the stage, and now it was time to deliver.

{Talk on Gratitude, Thankfulness, and Appreciation}

*"Thank you for this opportunity to be with you this evening. I am often humbled by the caliber of people I have the fortune to speak with, and this is the pinnacle of such an occasion. As I say what I'm going to say tonight, I'm actually not sure what you are going to get from it, as that will be entirely up to you. I've learned that **inspiration is not what I tell you, it's what you tell you.** So, tonight I invite you to listen with both your ears and your hearts for that little something that a higher source would have you attain as a result of this talk."*

"I noticed some of you have a notepad out, perhaps ready to grade me on my performance and contextual relevancy, and I just want to give a gentle reminder that I am not one of your students delivering my final doctoral thesis."

(A ripple of laughter and smiles spread through the crowd which lightened up the atmosphere, or rather biosphere, considerably.)

"I actually have a lot of history of my own here in Tucson. My father graduated from Amphitheater High School here where he was the student body president; then he went on to study at the University of Arizona where he met my mother. My ninety six years young grandfather still lives here, along with my aunt and uncle and several cousins."

"Years ago I attended Northern Arizona University and have competed against your tennis team, several times at this university. And for those competitive spirits in the room, I will leave you no longer in suspense to know that the U. of A. was victorious on every occasion."

(An even more jovial reaction scattered among the attendees).

"Perhaps I can introduce the topic tonight by relating an experience of an Austrian neurologist and psychiatrist who was also a Holocaust survivor. This gentleman chose to live by a philosophy that was an essential component to his survival. In his own words, he is known for saying, **'Everything can be taken from a man but one thing: the last of the human freedoms—to choose one's attitude in any given set of circumstances, to choose one's own way.'**

"You see, while the other holocaust victims were cursing the soldiers who were ordered to carry out the unspeakable actions, this man decided to thank them and bless them. When being served dinner, if you could call it that—since it typically consisted of some form of lukewarm water with some leaves and perhaps the undesirable parts of a fish—he would express his sincere gratitude for both the food and the soldier who provided it. He seemed to understand something about when we put our minds in a state of appreciation, it continues to live on, whereas a state of hatred and pessimism can often lead to death quicker than the sword or other physical ailments. He is also remembered for saying, 'When we are no longer able to change a situation, we are challenged to change ourselves.'

"He authored many bestsellers, but perhaps the one we know best is Man's Search for Meaning. *I am grateful for this man, Viktor Frankl, who proved his gratitude theory and lived*

to tell the story."

"*Not too far from here, another successful author, Gregg Braden, relates an experience on the authority of gratitude in his own words:*

(I pulled out the printed story and began to read.)

""*Back in the early '90s, I was living in the high desert of northern New Mexico. This was during one of the worst droughts that the Southwest had ever recorded. The elders in the native pueblos said that as far back as they could remember they'd never gone so long without rain.*

""*David, a Native American friend of mine from one of those nearby pueblos, called me one summer morning and asked if I wanted to join him in visiting a place his ancestors had built, where he would pray for rain. I agreed, and soon we were hiking through hundreds of acres of high desert sage. He led me to a place where there was a stone circle that reminded me of a medicine wheel. Each stone had been placed precisely by the hands of his ancestors long ago.*

""*I had an expectation of what I thought I was going to see. But my friend simply removed his hiking boots, then stepped with his naked feet into the stone circle. The first thing he did was honor all of his ancestors. Then he held his hands in a prayer position in front of his chest, turned his back to me, and closed his eyes. Less than a minute later, he turned around and said, "I'm hungry. Let's go get a bite to eat."*

""*Surprised, I said, "I thought you came here to pray for rain." I had been expecting to see some chanting and dancing.*

""*He looked at me and said, "No. If I prayed for rain, the rain could never happen."*

""*When I asked him why, he said it's because the moment you pray for something to occur, you've just acknowledged that it's not existing in that moment—and you may actually be denying the very thing you'd like to bring forward in your prayers.*

""*Well, if you didn't pray for rain just now when you closed your eyes," I said, "what did you do?"*

""*He said, "When I closed my eyes, I felt the feeling of what it feels like after there's been so much rain that I can stand with my naked feet in the mud of my pueblo village. I smelled the smells of rainwater rolling off the earthen walls of our homes. And I felt what it feels like to walk through a field of corn that is chest high because of all the rain that has fallen. In that way, I plant a seed for the possibility of that rain, and then I give thanks of gratitude and appreciation."*

'*I said, "You mean gratitude for the rain that you've created?"*

'*And he said, "No, we don't create the rain. I'm giving thanks of gratitude and appreciation for the opportunity to commune with the forces of creation."*

https://bolstablog.wordpress.com/2009/11/17/braden-prayer/

(I peered out to the audience to see their silent interpretation of what I just read. Some were nodding in agreement, and others were taking notes due to their "ah hah" moments.)

(I continued . . .)

"Isn't it interesting that David, Gregg's Native American friend, put himself in a state of genuine gratitude of what he wanted as if it had already taken place, instead of asking for it? Well, I should let you know that by the time they returned back to the pueblo, the rain had started coming down. The author admitted that this experience deepened his understanding of universal laws and completely transformed the way he prays.

"The incredible effects of this thing we call gratitude has a fair amount of research attached to it. Allow me to share a few of my findings.

"A neuroscientist at UCLA named Alex Korb compiled some notable research in an article he wrote titled, ""The Grateful Brain.""

(I pulled out the article and began to read a few of the highlights)

*"One study by a couple of American researchers' assigned young adults to keep a daily journal of things they were grateful for (Emmons & McCullough, 2003). They assigned other groups to journal about things that annoyed them, or reasons why they were better off than others. **The young adults assigned to keep gratitude journals showed greater increases in determination, attention, enthusiasm and energy compared to the other groups.** While that shows a clear benefit of gratitude, it also makes a clear distinction. **Realizing that other people are worse off than you is not gratitude**. Gratitude requires an appreciation of the positive aspects of your situation. It is not a comparison. Sometimes noticing what other people don't have*

may help you see what you can be grateful for, but you have to take that next step. **You actually have to show appreciation for what you have for it to have an effect.**

"Another study did not require a gratitude journal, but simply looked at the amount of gratitude people tended to show in their daily lives (Ng et al, 2012). In this study, a group of Chinese researchers looked at the combined effects of gratitude and sleep, quality on symptoms of anxiety and depression. They found that higher levels of gratitude were associated with better sleep, and with lower anxiety and depression. This begged the question, is the level of gratitude improving these symptoms or is it the fact that the patients are getting better sleep? These researchers ran some analyses controlling for the amount of sleep and revealed some interesting links.

"They found that after controlling for the amount of sleep people got, gratitude still had an effect on lower depression scores. This means that regardless of their levels of insomnia, people who showed more gratitude were less depressed. With anxiety they found a different result. After controlling for sleep, gratitude showed no effect on anxiety. So while higher gratitude led to less anxiety originally, this is simply because it helped people sleep better, and sleeping better improved their anxiety. So gratitude had a direct effect on depression symptoms (the more gratitude, the less depression) and an indirect effect on anxiety (increased gratitude led to improved sleep, which led to lower anxiety).

"Dr. Korb concludes that either way, with gratitude you're better off, and you get a good night's sleep.

"The final study comes from the National Institutes of Health (NIH). NIH researchers examined blood flow in various brain regions while subjects summoned up feelings of gratitude

(Zahn et al, 2009). They found that subjects who showed more gratitude overall had higher levels of activity in the hypothalamus. As you may already know, this is important because the hypothalamus controls a huge array of essential bodily functions, including eating, drinking, and sleeping. It also has a huge influence on your metabolism and stress levels. From this evidence on brain activity, it starts to become clear how improvements in gratitude could have such wide-ranging effects from increased exercise and improved sleep to decreased depression and fewer aches and pains.

"Furthermore, feelings of gratitude directly activated brain regions associated with the neurotransmitter dopamine. Dopamine feels good to get, which is why it's generally considered the 'reward' neurotransmitter. But dopamine is also important in initiating action. That means increases in dopamine make you more likely to do the thing you just did. It's the brain saying, 'Oh, do that again.'

https://www.psychologytoday.com/blog/prefrontal-nudity/201211/the-grateful-brain

(I placed Dr. Korb's article on the podium and continued...)

"Now that we have some documented research that clearly states the positive effects, you might ask, what are some immediate things one can do to live in a higher state of gratitude?

"A few years ago, a friend of mine, Steven Shallenberger, authored a book, Becoming Your Best: The 12 Principles of Highly Successful Leaders. *He relates that many successful people show their gratitude by hand-writing personal thank-you notes every week.*

"I knew this was something I could implement, so I

determined I would write three personal thank-you notes every Sunday. I went to the store and bought a box of blank thank-you cards, and put the repeating task to complete those notes on my calendar with an accompanying alert to remind me. There is no set pattern on who receives the grateful notes; rather, I go throughout my week with a gratitude radar and I always seem to know to whom I should write them. The results have been amazing. In a sense it is a form of a gratitude journal while lifting others as well. I've been doing this for almost three years now, and I have kept track of who I've sent them to on a spreadsheet. The long list includes family members, fellow church goers, work colleagues, friends, and others.

"It is remarkable how a simple little expression on a hand written note can fortify so many great relationships and have such a powerful impact. I can safely say I'm hooked on writing thank-you notes."

(I gazed out to observe the body language of the audience and assess if they would commit to putting this simple habit into action.)

"You know, this Biosphere has a lesson of gratitude of its own. As many of you probably already know, there has been a history of falling trees inside this manufactured and perfect environment. They grow remarkably fast, but because they have not developed a thing called 'reaction wood' or 'stress wood' in their roots, they can eventually topple over. A tree can only develop this reaction wood when the wind blows or the outside environment becomes adverse. Thus, because there is no wind inside the Biosphere, there is no strength for these trees to endure. **The point is, NO tree in its right state would ever curse the wind; rather it is grateful for it and it relies on it to become stronger.** When there is no wind, no tree can stand long term.

"How does this apply to us as humans? Can we look at the metaphoric winds and adverse conditions in our personal lives and say thank you for them, acknowledging that they will only make us stronger? This brings to the table the point that we benefit significantly when we choose to sincerely appreciate both the good and the challenging in our lives.

"This word appreciation is an interesting word that carries a lot of meaning. I think of a piece of real estate, for example. When a home appreciates, it obviously increases in value. If it depreciates, it decreases in value. Probably like many of you, we've owned a few homes and we've made it a point to love and care for them so the value increases. I've learned that the same model holds true for a person. **When a person 'appreciates' all that they have in their life, their personal value goes up.** Likewise on the flip side, when someone 'depreciates' or doesn't appreciate the people and things in their lives, their personal value goes down.

"While on a religious service mission in South America, I had a companion that was the epitome of someone who knows how to appreciate. He was from Colombia and came from very humble circumstances. In fact, every piece of clothing he wore was given to him. I know this because every morning—and I mean every morning—after he was dressed he would express his gratitude for everything he had on in this manner: "I'm so grateful to this person for giving me this shirt. That family gave me these pants, and I love them for it. This missionary gave me his tie and his shoes and blessed my life. That person gave me this belt and these socks, and I'll always be grateful."

"So I did what any smart person would do: I contributed to his wardrobe so he would start mentioning me in his daily *ritual of thanks."*

(Some of the audience were caught off guard and burst into laughter.)

"Interesting enough I came to realize that because this companion expressed his gratitude so sincerely and so often, he was constantly attracting more of what he was thankful for. He was always happy, always had a positive attitude, and was very successful in his labors. His value, although not materially high, outranked the rest of us by far because of his attitude of gratitude and appreciation."

(I paused and let silence fill the room so each person there could receive the message that was intended for him or her.)

"May you all be blessed in your efforts to be more grateful for all things and circumstances. I truly appreciate you coming this evening, and for this opportunity to give this talk. Thank you."

The audience offered a genuine and robust applause this time, and some approached me to tell me of the lessons they learned from the talk. One gentleman in particular said he was not expecting to feel the way he did, and that this talk was exactly what he needed. He felt like the message was meant specifically for him. His life had been full of challenges and he had been looking at these experiences as a curse instead of an opportunity to grow. After hearing my talk, he decided to change his perspective and he was already feeling better. And, as the research indicated, he said he was excited to get a good night's sleep and have his anxiety reduced.

Most of the audience had cleared the room, but I noticed Friedrich was still sitting in his chair with his arms folded patiently while he waited to speak with me. "How are you doing,

Friedrich?" I approached.

He sat there in silence, contemplating his response to me. After a moment, he finally said, "Is zis schubject of gratitude a schapter in your book?"

"It sure is," I responded with no hesitation. Again he was silent, and with a pensive look on his face and arms still folded he began nodding his head. I too folded my arms, started to nod my head, and looked at him as if to say, "Your move."

Finally, he asked in his thick German accent, "Vat is zee next schapter in your book, Thomas?" It was a harmless question, but his curious tone was giving me an uneasy feeling about this whole conversation.

"I'm actually not sure yet," I confessed.

"Vy is zat?" Without me realizing it, Friedrich's interrogation was leading me straight into telling him about Dr. Wright's notes and the course of the book.

All I could think to say was, "I'm still figuring that out."

Maintaining his calm demeanor, he asked, "Vould you mind schowing me zee book, and perhaps any notes zat you are drawing from?"

How did he know I had notes to draw from, and why would he be asking to see them? I wanted to show that I was not shaken up about all of this, so I casually replied, "I don't have the book with me, and I of course have been gathering research, but I don't have that with me either."

He immediately resorted to his posture of folded arms and head nodding as if to say, "I know more than you think I know."

When I told him I didn't have the book with me, I meant

it was not in my hands in that moment. The fact was that both the book and Dr. Wright's notes were zipped up in my computer bag over by the podium, but for some reason I was not comfortable sharing that with Friedrich.

I wanted to flee from the grasp of Friedrich's questioning, so I extended my hand and thanked him for coming tonight. I smiled and started slowly stepping backward. "You'll just have to purchase the book when it comes out," I said in an attempt to lighten the situation. Still wanting to maintain my poise, I casually walked over to pick up my bag and started making my way to the exit. I was not going to be detoured, and I made sure no one was following me.

Even though I knew it was late in Virginia, I called Kimberly on my way to the hotel. She answered with a tired voice but was delighted that all went well with my talk. I let her know I would be home tomorrow night, and we prayed together over the phone.

Once back at my hotel I called Clem; I wanted to let him know how it went and to tell him about Friedrich. Unfortunately, he did not answer, so I left him a message to call me back. I sat at my hotel room desk and let my mind focus on my gratitude for the wonderful night. I pulled out the book and opened it to where I had left off. I felt like there was a little more to say on the matter of gratitude, appreciation, and thankfulness.

With a prayer in my heart, I opened my copy of the King James Bible to the book of Luke, chapter 17, and after reading I began to summarize the well-known story found in verses 11–19.

As the Savior was traveling to Jerusalem, He passed through Samaria and Galilee. While passing through a certain village He was met by ten men who were lepers. They lifted up their voices and said, "Jesus, Master, have mercy on us."

When Jesus saw them He said unto them, "Go shew yourselves unto the priests." All ten went and were cleansed. However, when one of them saw that he was healed, he turned back, and with a loud voice glorified God. He fell down on his face, giving the Savior thanks. And Jesus said, "Were there not ten cleansed, but where are the nine? They are not found that returned to give glory to God, save this stranger." Then Jesus said to the man who returned to give thanks, "Go thy way, thy faith hath made thee whole."

I can only imagine how all these men must have felt to have been healed from this terrible, reprehensible disease. In this account, only one man returned to personally thank Jesus for His miraculous gift of healing. The Savior then pronounced an additional blessing on the grateful man. My feeling is that the other nine who were cured from leprosy were also very grateful. However, the Lord recognized the one who returned to verbally express gratitude.

We see that the greater blessing lies with those who take the time and effort to express their gratitude, appreciation, and thankfulness.

Start your Gratitude Journal by writing down ten things and/or people for which you are grateful:

1._____

2._____

3._____

4._____

5._____

6._____

7._____

8. _____

9._____

10._____

Chapter 9

The Liberating Language of Forgiveness

I had one final stop in Tucson before I headed back to Virginia, and that was to visit Poppy—Garrett Eugene Blackwell, my paternal grandfather. I am always amazed at how sharp his mind is even at the age of ninety-six. Though he is a man of few words, he does not miss any details.

As I pulled into the parking lot of the active retirement facility where Poppy lived my phone was buzzing. Clem was calling me back. *"Hola mi amigo, como estas?"* I greeted.

"Muy bien, but yo hablo muy poquito espanish," Clem attempted. "Sorry I missed your call; how's everything going, and how'd it go at Biosphere 2? We heard from my father's colleague that your talk was incredible!"

"I felt it went well, and I am very grateful," I recounted. "But I met a man named Friedrich from Germany there who was asking me a lot of pointed questions."

"What kind of questions?" Clem probed curiously.

"Questions that would make me believe he knew something about the book and the notes," I described with concern in my voice.

"Okay, Thomas, I'll let my father know," Clem retorted abruptly with no further explanation.

I wasn't really satisfied with his answer, but I also didn't have a lot of time to discuss it right then.

"Clem, before you hang up, I wanted to ask your permission about something? I'm about to go visit my grandfather, and I wondered if it would be all right if I showed him the book and Dr. Wright's notes? I feel there would be no harm in this, and truth be told, I really don't know how much longer he'll be with us."

"All right, you can show him as long as you feel it is safe," Clem consented.

"Thank you, I do feel it is safe. Is there anything else I need to know about?" I asked.

"Nothing for now; just keep writing and I will be in touch soon."

I made my way up the elevator and knocked at Poppy's third-floor apartment door. I heard a faint voice reply, "Come on in." There he sat in his favorite recliner chair looking out the window with several books stacked beside him.

"Hi there cowboy, how are you?" Poppy tenderly greeted me the same way he had since I was old enough to wear one of his old cowboy hats. I immediately went over and gave him a big hug.

"What you got there?" he inquired.

"This is actually a book I am writing, and I wanted to tell you about it," I confided.

"Oh, what kind of book?"

"It is a book about how our words create our reality. Essentially, we bring about what we talk about," I described.

"Oh, that's interesting. It sounds fancy," he mused.

"Poppy, very few people know I am writing this, but I wanted to share it with you. It has some ties back to WWII and some German U-boat soldiers who were captured and housed in a jail in Boston that was renovated into a luxurious hotel. The book is going to be called *The Liberty of Our Language Revealed.*"

I could see his left eyebrow raise as I piqued his interest with the subject matter. Poppy had fought in WWII as a pilot, and throughout my life had related a few war stories to me. I felt comfortable sharing some of the confidential intricacies with him, so I told him about Dr. Maxwell Wright and his notes.

"What's the next chapter going to be on?" he asked.

"Actually I am not sure. I need to read what the next page of notes says."

"Well, what are you waiting for cowboy? Why don't you look at the next page?" Poppy asked with a friendly yet demanding voice. At his insistence I pulled out page 6 of Dr. Wright's notes. Poppy leaned forward in his chair and put his best ear forward to hear.

The Liberating Language of Forgiveness

Nothing will liberate a person more than their willingness to forgive another and let go wholeheartedly of any wrongs that might have been committed. And nothing will impede a person's progression more in this life than an unwillingness to forgive another of their trespasses. Holding grudges or harboring ill feelings toward another person/people, organization, or even a political party far removes us from our infinite potential to succeed. Additionally, the one who has the discipline to ask for forgiveness and express the words "I'm sorry" immediately opens the door to greater possibilities. Relationships in all their forms will be stronger; Peace and vitality will be more present in one's life.

I gazed up at my wise grandfather to see his reaction to what I just read. He leaned back in his recliner and clasped his hands together then put them up to his lips. He was in a deep contemplative state and for some time, no words were spoken by either of us.

"That is a true statement," Poppy said, finally breaking the silence. A memory flashed into my mind of when Poppy showed compassion to a stranger many years ago when I was just a boy.

We were visiting my grandparents' home in Tucson when there was a knock at the door. My brothers must have been in another part of the house, because I remember being in the front room alone watching Poppy open the door. It was a young man from Mexico who spoke little English. He had just come across the border looking for work and was very hungry. I saw my grandfather make him a sack lunch, and through the large window in the front room I watched as he walked with him, explaining that he was very sorry that he had no work to offer.

In the end Poppy put his hand on the young man's shoulder and wished him the best on his journey. Sincere smiles were exchanged, and Poppy returned and explained to me what had just happened. Even at a young age, I remember understanding that Poppy was not offended by or scared of this stranger; rather, he showed love and compassion. The young man was likely in our country undocumented, but Poppy saw him as a person needing help regardless of his circumstance.

"Hand me that Bible there, Tommy," Poppy said, interrupting my blast from the past. He held the sacred book like a dear old friend with whom he had gone through many of life's experiences. He knew exactly what he was looking for as he opened to the book of Matthew, chapter 18, then returned the Bible to me directing me to read starting with verse 21. Poppy returned to his comfortable position leaning back in his chair, hands clasped and resting against his chin. He was waiting for me to read the highlighted verses.

I began.

21 Then came Peter to him, and said, Lord, how oft shall my brother sin against me, and I forgive him? till seven times?

22 Jesus saith unto him, I say not unto thee, Until seven times: but, Until seventy times seven.

23 Therefore is the kingdom of heaven likened unto a certain king, which would take account of his servants.

24 And when he had begun to reckon, one was brought unto him, which owed him ten thousand talents.

25 But forasmuch as he had not to pay, his lord commanded him to be sold, and his wife, and children, and all that he had, and payment to be made.

26 The servant therefore fell down, and worshipped him, saying, Lord, have patience with me, and I will pay thee all.

27 Then the lord of that servant was moved with compassion, and loosed him, and forgave him the debt.

28 But the same servant went out, and found one of his fellow servants, which owed him an hundred pence: and he laid hands on him, and took him by the throat, saying, Pay me that thou owest.

29 And his fellow servant fell down at his feet, and besought him, saying, Have patience with me, and I will pay thee all.

30 And he would not: but went and cast him into prison, till he should pay the debt.

31 So when his fellow servants saw what was done, they were very sorry, and came and told unto their lord all that was done.

32 Then his lord, after that he had called him, said unto him, O thou wicked servant, I forgave thee all that debt, because thou desiredst me:

33 Shouldest not thou also have had compassion on thy fellow servant, even as I had pity on thee?

34 And his lord was wroth, and delivered him to the tormentors, till he should pay all that was due unto him.

35 So likewise shall my Heavenly Father do also unto you, if ye from your hearts forgive not every one his brother their trespasses.

I waited to hear what Poppy might say in response to my reading from these life-guiding verses. A tear welled up in his left eye as he began, "Tommy, I've done my best to follow these principles throughout my life. I've had many opportunities to forgive in big situations, and in turn be forgiven both by people and by God."

His heartfelt words went straight to my core, as I was already familiar with some of those "big" situations. A little choked up, I responded, "Me too, Poppy, me too."

"To err is human, to forgive, divine." —Alexander Pope

"How about we go get some dinner, Tommy?"

"Sure, that would be great," I concurred.

We made our way down the hallway to the elevator and arrived at the first floor. Poppy got around with a walker but still had great strength. For as long as I could remember, in his earlier years, he woke up early and went for a run then retreated to his office and read from the Bible. He was a tremendous example of discipline and discipleship.

While waiting in line at the retirement community cafeteria, Poppy turned his attention to a sweet lady sitting near us. "You see that gal over there? Her name is Helen, and I enjoy her companionship at dinner. She's 105 years old." My eyes widened and jaw dropped in reaction to that new bit of information.

All of a sudden, Poppy was calling in a rather loud voice to his dinner friend. "C'mon, Helen, it's time for dinner!" Helen caught a glimpse of Poppy and began rocking back and forth to both get out of her chair and reach her walker, which was a short distance in front of her. For what seemed like an eternity, yet was probably just a few seconds, Poppy and I watched Helen struggle to get out of her chair and reach that walker. I couldn't take it anymore and impulsively started heading in Helen's direction. Anticipating my actions, Poppy grabbed my forearm to stop me from providing her any assistance.

"You let her get it Tommy. She'll get it," Poppy told me.

His attention was again turned to the struggling 105-year young woman. "C'mon, Helen, you can do it!"

Suddenly, like a wild fire, the entire line of residents in the cafeteria, all using walkers, joined their support in yelling (everyone yelled in this place), "C'mon, Helen, you can do it!" As Helen finally made it to her walker, a cheer broke out, and with that she was heading in our direction. I wanted to record the whole thing, as I felt like I was in a triumphant scene from a movie. I instinctively pulled out my phone and took a picture of this victorious lady.

Helen, age 105

This was a moment not to be forgotten, and I was eager to note the lessons learned from this experience in the book.

During dinner we had a very pleasant conversation. Helen loved to talk, and she loved to eat. Interesting enough, she ate more than both Poppy and I. The time came when I had to ask the big question—the question that only Helen had the authority to answer, but I still wondered if she would know how to respond.

"Helen, do you mind if I ask you a personal question?" I respectfully asked.

"Of course, you can ask me anything you want. As long as you are alright with me answering any way I want." Helen responded with a twinkle in her eye.

"What's your secret, Helen? What's the secret to living a long, happy, fulfilled life?"

Without any hesitation she began to answer. "Many, many, many years ago, I consciously decided not to waste any of my time or energy getting mad or angry at people or situations. I chose not to be offended any more. If people did me wrong, I freely and quickly forgave them, with no grudges. Likewise, if I made a mistake and potentially offended another, I quickly asked for their forgiveness."

A little taken back with her answer, I looked at Poppy to see if he heard what Helen just told me. A gentle head nod and faint smile signified he had. Her answer was incredible and right in line with the topic at hand. She continued with confidence, "I believe this has added years to my life and bliss to my days."

"Thank you for sharing that insight, Helen. Do you then believe that when people do hold grudges or spend time being angry that life is literally being shortened for them?" I asked.

"I believe so. That is my feeling anyway," she wisely responded.

Just then Poppy put a cap on the conversation. "Well, Tommy, looks like you have some more material for your book."

"I believe you're right, Poppy. Thank you, Helen, you've been most insightful. Do you mind if we take a picture together?" They both agreed.

With Helen and Poppy Blackwell; she let me sit on her walker

After a tender goodbye, I went to my car and pulled out the book and began to write my thoughts on what Helen said about forgiving quickly, and the lessons I learned from her struggling to reach her walker.

Our bodies and spirits are not meant to house ill feelings towards others. It's like lighting a fire inside of a house and letting it burn without taking any action to put it out. Inevitably there is going to be a lot of damage to that house, and if no action is taken to put it out, the fire may even completely destroy it.

{Power Paragraphs}

{When this beautiful, wise lady finally rocked out of her chair and reached her walker, I realized something. **There is necessity and majesty contained in our struggles**. Sure, I could have easily walked over and helped Helen out of her chair, but that would have increased her dependency and weakened the inner will as well as muscles needed to stand on her own. Internally, Helen knew that if she could stand on her own, she would have another day on this glorious earth.

Poppy certainly understood this as he grabbed my arm, forbidding me to provide her assistance. His help and the aid of her friends cheering in the cafeteria line came through, shouting **words of encouragement and support.** Then came the glorious recognition when Helen finally stood up out of her chair and reached her walker. We often think we are supporting and helping someone by doing a task for them. However, the opposite effect of debilitating dependency can result. I've heard it said that **"We cannot do another's push-ups for them."**}

After noting my thoughts, I headed for the airport to get back to the east coast, where my sweet family was anxiously waiting. While at the airport I stopped by a book store to start looking at the current titles and genres on the best sellers list. I had never really paid much attention to this before, but now that I was working on this movement, it piqued my interest.

Near the entrance, there was a box of random books. For some reason, I was drawn to these books that were perhaps not in the limelight anymore. I began to sift through the pile to see if any caught my attention. Then an unexpected book title was in my hands, and I couldn't seem to put it down. *Prisoners are People* was written by Kenyon J. Scudder, and the introduction read:

A record of a courageous, humane, and rewarding experiment which points the way to a new orientation in prison work and the regenerative results possible, based on Prison Warden Kenyon Scudder's experience in the new prison at Chino, California, which was set up in 1940. Determined to head a minimum security prison, Scudder did away with fences, watch towers and armed guards, selected his personnel with care, and handpicked his prisoners from San Quentin who were given a freedom within walls based on trust and responsibility. Here are all the aspects of prison life in Chino; the food—much of which they raised themselves; their part in the war effort, canning beef for the Army, and in the forestry camp nearby; the educational and trade training program which prepared the men for a more secure, economic future; the recreation, which included parties at the Scudders' house. A story of progressive penology which reflects the confidence and the conviction of a man who believed in his methods and his men, with warm interest.

Drawn in by this introduction, I bought the book for $19.95.

Before boarding the plane, I called Kimberly to let her know I was coming home. Her voice sounded a little more solemn than normal. "Oh, honey, I'm afraid I have some sad news," she said.

"What is it? Is everything all right?"

"Yes, we are okay, but we just got word that Patrick passed away. They are having the funeral this Saturday, and his wife told me that his last request was to have you speak and to have Makayla read a favorite poem of his at the service," Kimberly explained.

"Oh, my dear pal Patrick. Bless your soul, my friend. Thank you for letting me know. I'll see you soon, sweetheart. I Love you."

As I hung up the phone, I reflected on my beloved friend Patrick. He was one of the kindest most loving men I had ever met. He often called me randomly, just to check on me, and every time before hanging up he said, "I love you, brother." The first couple of times it caught me off guard, but then I realized that he was going to say it every time, without fail, so I embraced it and began to return the sentiment. Patrick truly did love people, and his affection for life and for others grew as he contracted cancer. He knew his time was limited, so he determined he was going to be a light to as many people as possible. Very few people knew he had cancer, including me, until just a couple months ago when he called me out of the blue and asked if I would say a prayer with him. I readily agreed, and when he arrived at our home I asked him what specifically he wanted to say a prayer for.

He said, "Oh, because I have cancer, and either I want it to go away, or I want to be able to handle what lies ahead." None of us had any idea of what he was dealing with. After the prayer, we both had a feeling that his time to leave this mortal earth was drawing near, but I knew it was his desire that I not share this with anyone.

At 35,000 feet I began to contemplate what I might say at Patrick's funeral. Many thoughts and memories raced through my mind. I felt a little inadequate, as I had known Patrick for only a couple of years. Yet, I knew much of his life story, and after all, he's the one who made the request. I considered who might attend the service—his beautiful, new, young wife; his bitter ex-wife and their two daughters; his estranged daughter from a previous relationship; his saintly brother; his church family; and his many loyal friends he gained while stepping in and out of re-hab.

Picturing the audience in my mind, I closed my eyes and imagined my dear friend Patrick sitting next to me. Up to this point in my life, I hadn't really made it a habit to talk with those who have passed on. However, I felt it was appropriate given the circumstance, so I rolled with it.

"Patrick, now that you've seen the other side of this mortal life, what would you want to say to all of these people? If you had one more chance to say something, what would it be?" I listened with reverence, and Patrick's response to my question graciously came. I noted his words down, and sat in humble reflection of the divine experience of somehow hearing the thoughts of my deceased friend. I was now clear on the message he wanted shared at his funeral, and I offered up a prayer of gratitude.

I looked at my watch and realized I had a lot more time left on this flight, so I pulled out the book I purchased at the airport and began to read. Warden Scudder definitely had a unique way of running a prison. Rather than strict guards and barbed wire fences, he chose love, service, and trusting inmates with responsibility to rehabilitation and openness to repentance. Based on the evidence in his book, his philosophy proved that people tend to act how we speak to and treat them. These two must be congruent, though. In other words, we cannot say, "I believe you have great potential and I trust you will do the right thing," only to lock you up and remove any opportunity to prove me right.

While reading this intriguing book, I came across a story that was the reason I believe the book would not leave my hands until I bought it. I took out my hardbound book and began to note it down.

As related by Kenyon J. Scudder:

A friend of mine happened to be sitting in a railroad coach next to a young man who was obviously depressed. Finally, the man revealed that he was a paroled convict returning from a distant prison. His imprisonment had brought shame to his family, and they had neither visited him nor written often. He hoped, however, that this was only because they were too poor to travel and too uneducated to write. He hoped, despite the evidence, that they had forgiven him.

To make it easy for them, however, he had written them to put up a signal for him when the train passed their little farm on the outskirts of town. If his family had forgiven him, they were to put a white ribbon in the big apple tree which stood near the tracks. If they didn't want him to return, they were to do nothing, and he would remain on the train as it traveled west to build a new life in a new city.

As the train neared his home town, the suspense became so great he couldn't bear to look out of his window. He exclaimed, "In just five minutes the engineer will sound the whistle indicating our approach to the long bend which opens into the valley I know as home. Will you watch for the apple tree at the side of the track?" His companion changed places with him and said he would. The minutes seemed like hours, but then there came the shrill sound of the train whistle. The young man anxiously asked, "Can you see the tree? Is there a white ribbon?"

Came the reply: "I see the tree. I see not one white ribbon, but many. There is a white ribbon on every branch. Son, someone surely does love you."

In that instant all the bitterness that had poisoned a life was dispelled. "I felt as if I had witnessed a miracle," the man said.

I wrote:

A miracle indeed! A miracle of forgiveness. Those of us who know what it's like to be forgiven of a past wrong, whether major or minor, understand some of what this former convict was feeling.

A few days later, I found myself sitting at a funeral in front of a diverse crowd, anticipating the talk I had been asked to give by Patrick prior to his passing. As odd as it may sound, I have always enjoyed going to funerals. They give me a renewed appreciation for the preciousness of life and a greater determination to live each day with purpose. Many of those present were visibly saddened by his passing. There were a few who showed up out of respect, yet it appeared that they were still harboring hurt feelings. I felt a sense of peace and confidence as I reflected on my experience on the plane when I felt Patrick had relayed his desired message to me.

{A Portion of the Talk I gave at Patrick's Funeral}

"Many of you might be wondering why I was asked to give this tribute to Patrick, and the answer is I'm not exactly sure why. We did have a fairly close relationship, and he felt comfortable sharing many of his life's experiences with me.

"We all know Patrick was very playful and rarely took himself too seriously. Recently, while heading into our local

supermarket, I noticed someone in the distance riding the back of a shopping cart through the parking lot like it was skateboard. Behind him I noticed a woman frantically running and yelling, 'Patrick you be careful!'"

(A ripple of hardy laughter from the audience broke up the solemnity of the occasion.)

"At the risk of being vulnerable, I will tell you that I struggled to know what to say today about this dear and loving friend of ours whose life we are honoring. I wished there was a way to interview him before he passed on about what message he might want to leave. Then recently while contemplating this talk, I got this impression to just ask Patrick as if he were still alive and sitting next to me. I closed my eyes, said a little prayer, then asked, 'Patrick what is it you want me to say at your funeral? What would you want us to know, now that you are on the other side?' I'm grateful that somehow the message that he would want us to know was communicated to me in my mind and heart. Here is what I heard, and if you are willing, close your eyes and imagine Patrick saying it."

(A sublime reverence hushed over the congregation as I gazed out and saw their eyes close in anticipation of what I was going to say next.)

"'All the worries, doubts, and hard feelings that plague us in life don't matter anymore over here. They just don't matter. It has painfully come to my knowledge all the time I wasted fretting the small offenses, and occasions I withheld my love from another due to petty grievances. My soul is deeply saddened because of this, and I wish I could get that time back. Please, please forgive each other freely.'"

(I paused for a long minute and allowed a moment of silence to let people feel whatever they were supposed to feel. The simple yet deep message sparked some audible sobs. Some hung their heads, and others put their hands over their faces to shield their emotion.)

"What a powerful and divine message from Patrick. Of all the things he could have told us, forgiveness was the most important message. I imagine many of you feel like he was speaking directly to you. Maybe he's also asking some of you to forgive him for whatever circumstances might be.

"We are all witnesses that while on this earth, this beautiful friend, father, brother, and husband of ours brought joy and blessings to our lives. I know he lives on, and I know we will reunite with him again someday. Let us all remember his counsel the rest of our days: Please, please, forgive each other freely."

"If we really want to love, we must learn how to forgive." —Mother Teresa

Choose to Forgive Today:

_____

_____

_____

_____

Chapter 10

When It Comes to Money Matters

It was so good to be back in Virginia with my beautiful wife and girls. Kimberly and I had some long conversations about my experiences in Tucson. This was one of those times where we lost track of time and found ourselves talking late into the night.

"What's next in the book?" she asked. Not really sure how to answer, I pulled out Dr. Wright's notes. "Do you mind if I look at what you've written so far?" Kimberly asked as she took the old leather notebook out of my hand.

"Well, I guess not."

"Wow, you've written quite a bit already. Good job!" She congratulated.

"Thank you. I'm grateful it is coming along."

She thumbed through the pages like a seasoned book critic. "Ooh, I like that—the rate of vibration of our daily greetings."

I let her leaf through what had been written so far and was pleased it met with her approval. "Okay, so what's next?" she asked again. I pulled out page 7 from the notes and began to read.

When It Comes to Money Matters

Are the words we use attracting or distracting money to flow into our life? Our relationship with money and its sources will manifest wealth, mediocrity, or even poverty. Many false traditions around negative money beliefs have been passed down from generation to generation, and one must be conscious if their words are supporting these false traditions.

We live in a world where the exchange of money is necessary. Those who embrace this knowledge will have more of it, and those who are afraid of it or condemn it will have less. Living a wealthy life means something different to everyone, and one must decide what it looks like for him or her. Money is a wonderful thing, and the more you have the more good you can do with it. However, it is not the true source of happiness, and its sole pursuit will leave one stranded on an unfulfilling island.

Kimberly smiled at me and said, "We've certainly experienced a roller coaster ride when it comes to money, haven't we!" I raised one eyebrow and took a deep breath to acknowledge what she was referencing. Then she glanced down at the book again and read aloud the last chapter title, "The Liberating Language of Forgiveness."

"Hey, we had an experience that will go along with both your last chapter and this one!" she said enthusiastically and without warning.

"Great, let's hear it."

"Remember when we had left the restaurant business, you had been working for almost two years in financial services, and we struggled terribly?"

It was painful to recall, and I nodded my head. "How could I forget?"

"You were working so hard and doing everything your managers asked you to do, yet it still seemed like nothing was really clicking for you. Then remember, I changed my prayer from asking for you to have success to whether there was anything I needed to change that might be holding us back from succeeding? Do you remember what my answer was?"

"I do you—" but before I could continue, she had already continued with the rest of the story.

"It came to me so clearly that I was holding on to hard feelings against one of the family members who owned the restaurant. I needed to forgive them first in order for us to succeed, so I determined I was going to call her the next day and apologize for having these negative feelings. I had to forgive her in my heart." With her mouth open, Kimberly paused to signify that she was on to something huge.

"Which you did . . ." I said to get the train back on the tracks.

"Which I did, and it seemed like very shortly thereafter we experienced enormous growth in your financial services business. Interesting, what was holding us back was my holding on to bitterness. People should really evaluate that in their lives! Don't you think that should go in the book?" Kimberly prodded.

"Umm, I'll see if it makes the cut . . ." I responded sarcastically.

"That's good material right there," she pressed.

"You're right, that is some good material," I said with no escape.

"You're welcome!" she said with a charming twinkle in her eye.

"Thank you, sweetheart, that's an incredible example and I will consider it," I committed.

"Any time you need some more material, just ask," she concluded.

Over the next several days I reflected on the topic at hand. Kimberly was certainly right when she mentioned our financial roller coaster. We had experienced highs and lows when it comes to income and money in the bank. That cycle had repeated itself a few times. Even though there had been some hard times, I knew financial abundance could be recreated over and over.

I was in high school when I first recognized the power of what Dr. Maxwell Wright alluded to in creating financial abundance. I started to notice how people who earned a significant amount of money spoke, in contrast to the language of those who didn't. Early in our marriage, I spent a considerable amount of time studying wealth patterns, and for many years have taught them to countless numbers of people.

I began to write.

The late Dr. Wayne Dyer described the amount of abundance we can obtain in the form of a metaphor. If the great and vast ocean represented abundance, does it really care how much we take from it? Yet many people show up to the ocean with a "lack" mentality. They have a thimble to fill because they don't want to take too much, or they want to make sure there is more tomorrow. Another person might show up with a wheelbarrow or two and take in a bit more than just a thimble full. Then there is the person who knows there is plenty, so they show up with semi-trucks with empty tanker trailers ready to fill. The lesson is, does our language and mindset represent a thimble, a wheelbarrow, or a semi-truck? The ocean will provide and fill each, so why not show up with a semi-truck?

What is your language when you see something you desire that costs a significant amount of money? Are you quick to eliminate the possibility by saying the debilitating words, "That's too expensive," or "I can't afford that?" Or, do you open the opportunity to make it yours by saying, **"I will figure out how to have that!"**

It's important to distinguish the difference between expensive and value. When someone says, "that's too expensive," all they are saying is that item is not worthy of their money and does not have enough value for them to purchase it. When we truly see value in something, we will pay the required amount. Those who go through life feeling that everything is too expensive, have lost their sense of seeing value and are heading down a "lack"-filled path.

The key is to know that you can obtain whatever you want, but you have to **dare to declare it, believe it, and**

then take the action necessary to achieve it. In short. **SAY, DO, ACHIEVE.** If we miss the first step of saying it, or if we say the antithesis of achieving the desired goal, there is little to no possibility of it ever coming into reality.

When Kimberly and I were I first married, we rode our bikes in a certain neighborhood and adored the gorgeous houses and the majestic large trees. **We talked as if we lived there.** We even toured one of the houses that came up for sale, and in our minds acted like we were already eligible to purchase it. Just a year and half later, we had earned enough money to be eligible to purchase a home in that price range. Another home on that same street came up for sale, and it happened to be our favorite. It was a yellow Victorian home with a wraparound porch. It had a swimming pool and a tennis court. What a great feeling it was to know we could buy it. However, we felt led to a completely different area in another city, where we bought an incredible home that was similarly priced.

I look back on that experience and recognize that our thoughts, words, and actions were congruent with achieving what we desired. I call this **Visionary Action Dreaming**. This is where you are willing to have a dream and a vision of what you want, and you are eager to take the required actions to achieve it. We have continued this pattern throughout our marriage.

One vision in particular that we put into action was to have Kimberly at home to nurture our children as a full-time homemaker. Although at times it was not easy financially, from the moment our first daughter was born, Kimberly has never earned another paycheck.

Times and seasons were marching on, and I had not heard from Clem for a few weeks. With the trees in full bloom,

Kimberly and I took the girls to one of our favorite spots in Richmond—Maymont Park. The pristine hundred-acre grounds, magnificent flower gardens, and Victorian mansion have been open to the public for nearly a century. James Henry and Sally May Dooley were the original owners and visionaries. We loved to stroll throughout the park's winding paths or sit on a blanket on the grass sheltered by one of its many immaculate shade trees.

I brought the book with me to write while in that inspired environment. I found a bench that faced the west side of the mansion just beneath a hovering oak tree. Kimberly was in the near distance with our three princesses, enjoying a picnic while sitting on a blanket cushioned by the picture-perfect grass.

I began to write.

Thank you, Mr. and Mrs. Dooley, for acting on an inspired dream and vision. Your big thinking has blessed a century of visitors and many more to come.

As I looked around at the different people meandering through the grounds, I had to wonder, are they inspired by the Dooleys' accomplishments to do something bigger in their lives? On the other hand, are they saying to themselves, "Wow, I'll never be able to have something like this!" Either way, they'll get what they entertain, and the fact that James Henry and Sally May achieved it, demonstrates that it is possible.

Incorporating into our language, **"If it's been done, it can be done,"** is an immediate opener of great possibilities. Are we enthused by people's accomplishments, or do we condemn those accomplishments because they are not ours?

I glanced up at my precious family laughing, soaking in the sun, and playing with our little Liberty May. What I felt was priceless. I realized my most prized possessions in my life were the things money could not buy. We were at a free park, surrounded by God's creations and enjoying the simple things.

I continued writing:

Happiness cannot be purchased with a certain amount of money. It comes from true fulfillment and an inner peace of conscience. *Temporary pleasures will subside. One must figure out how to be happy with or without money.*

I know the feeling of not providing well for my family, and there is no inner peace of conscience when that is the case. Like Dr. Wright wrote, "We live in a world where the exchange of money is necessary. Those who embrace this knowledge will have more of it, and those that are afraid of it or condemn it will have less." If it is my choice, which I know it is, I choose to embrace this knowledge and have more of it!

I put down my pen and inhaled the fresh air while stretching out my arms. I could feel my phone buzzing in my pocket. It was Clem.

"Is this *the* Clemson James Michael Wright?" I quipped.

"Stop that! You sound like my mother when I've done something wrong," Clem said as he laughed.

"Great to hear from you brother, I was wondering when we were going to connect again. It's been several weeks," I continued.

"Yeah, nothing had come up and I wanted to give you some space to write. I do have something for you now, though. One of the largest and most successful network marketing companies in the world is having an annual convention in Las

Vegas, and you are going to be one of their keynote speakers," Clem explained.

"Wow, okay. When is it?"

"It's in three weeks, and there will be more than twenty thousand people in attendance. Can you handle that Mr. Blackwell?"

"Of course I can!"

"Also, before you ask me what you're supposed to talk on, it's your choice. I'll be sending more details a little later."

"Perfect, sounds great. Anything else I should know?"

"No, you already know too much," he replied lightheartedly.

I spent the next few weeks preparing a talk that I felt would inspire the large audience. I wanted to fit it in line with my current chapter, "When It Comes to Money Matters."

When I arrived at the Las Vegas airport, there was a gentleman standing at the bottom of the escalator wearing a black jacket, a pair of jeans, and a polo shirt with a sign that said "Welcome Mr. T. Blackwell." On the bottom of the sign was written the name of the organization I was speaking for, so I knew it was for me.

"Hi there, I'm Mr. T. Blackwell, how are you my friend?"

The chauffeur smiled and said with a strong accent, "Fery gut, another day in paradize." I don't know why, but something did not feel right. What kind of chauffeur wears a suit jacket and jeans? And that accent seems to be popping up a lot lately. "May I take your bag for you, zir?" he beckoned.

"No thank you, I'm good," I declined, as I knew the book and notes were in there.

He led me, with no conversation, from the baggage claim down to the lower level of the parking garage and a waiting black Lincoln Town Car. My cell phone kept vibrating. Someone was calling, but my hands were full and I couldn't get to it. He held the back door open, waiting for me to get in.

"Do you mind if I put my bag in the trunk?" I asked.

His eyes peered at the trunk. "No, zee trunk is full right now." That didn't make sense; why would his trunk be full when he conveys people and luggage for a living?

My phone buzzed again, this time with a new text message. I glanced at my phone; it was from Clem. "Thomas, take only public transportation, our operation has been compromised!"

Glancing up at the imposter who realized he had been discovered, I immediately bolted for the airport terminal, wheeling my suitcase and running as fast as I could.

Not wanting to be caught or noticed, the mysterious man jumped in the executive car and sped away.

My heart was racing at the prospect of me getting into the fake chauffer's car and him taking me to who knows where! I stayed in the baggage claim area which was heavily occupied with people, and sat against the wall where I could see everything around me. After about thirty minutes, I went over to the public transportation line, hailed a taxi, and took it to the hotel on the strip where the event was being held.

The moment I got in my hotel room, I called Clem. "Hey, what's going on? I was seriously almost kidnapped at the airport by some guy posing as a chauffeur. He had my name on a sign."

"Are you all right?" Clem asked.

"Yes, I'm all right, but that was crazy. Who is after me, and what has been compromised?"

"My father received an anonymous phone call from someone saying he knows who we are, and who you are, and that they know about this whole movement. They are not out to hurt anyone; they just want the notes and the book," Clem explained.

"Who are they? Did your father mention anything about the anonymous caller having a foreign accent?"

"No, nothing about an accent, and I am not sure who they are. I just know we will have to continue to use extreme caution. Thomas, it is better that you are always in public areas when outside your hotel room. Look, Thomas, this is obviously a big deal, or whoever this opposing force is wouldn't care about it. Go give your talk tomorrow, and we will be in touch."

As soon as I hung up with Clem my hotel room phone rang. I hesitated, wondering if I should answer.

"Hello?" I said faintly.

I felt somewhat comforted that the person on the other line did not have a foreign accent similar to that of my fake chauffeur. His accent was definitely from somewhere in the South though.

"Hi there, this is Gene Beverly; we spoke earlier when making your travel arrangements. Some of the key executives and I were fixin' to go to dinner and we'd love for you to join us."

"I'd love that, Gene, thank you."

"Great; we'll meet you outside in front of the hotel at 7pm."

We all piled into a large limousine, and headed for dinner. I was introduced to several of the executives of the company. "What are you planning on talking about tomorrow Thomas?" one executive wasted no time in asking.

"That depends what the audience needs to hear," I responded with a grin. "What can you tell me about the attendees?"

Another executive took the opportunity to answer. "In our company, and often times in this whole industry, you'll find those that are doing extremely well, those that are on the cusp of doing extremely well, those who are making just enough to go full time, and the largest group are those who are fairly new and excited for the possibility of doing extremely well." He looked around the rest of the car to his fellow executives and asked, "Does that sound about right?"

A myriad of head nods followed with responses of "Yep that sounds about right" echoed throughout the stretch limousine.

"Great, thank you. That helps me understand your group better."

As we entered the prestigious restaurant an interesting experience happened. We were about to be escorted to our table when an unruly entourage approached the reservation desk. I glanced over to see as people were pointing fingers and whispering the name of the person in the center of the group. Sure enough, it was a Major League Baseball superstar.

The hostess recognized who he was and said, "I will be

right with you, sir." In an instant, the character of this famous athlete was exposed. Using a rude and abrupt voice, he said, "Do you even know who I am?" A trickle of laughter spewed from his groupies.

A little taken back, but still with confidence, the hostess replied, "I have an idea who are you are, sir; do you have a reservation?"

"No, I shouldn't need a reservation. Don't you think I've earned the right to not need a reservation?" His tone was abusive, and looked back at his entourage, seeking their approval.

"I'm sorry, sir, with all due respect, we have a fully reserved restaurant this evening, and I'd be happy to put you on a waiting list," said the hostess keeping her composure.

"A waiting list!? Nobody puts me on a wait list! You see these rings with all these diamonds? Do you have any idea what these mean!?" His voice raised, he was making quite a scene as he flashed his World Series rings in the hostess's face.

Then it happened. It couldn't have been more perfect. The hostess rounded her shoulders, took a deep breath, looked that arrogant millionaire in the face, and said in a clear, direct tone, "Look. You make the money, but the money does not make you, and I would suggest that with all that money, you invest in some people skills." She silenced him with her great choice in words, and he and his obnoxious group stormed out of the restaurant.

She then turned to our group and said, "Right this way to your table, please." We all impulsively applauded her performance and followed her. Dinner that evening was great, but no subsequent detail would top the message and the manner of that hostess.

"Circumstance does not make the man, it reveals him." —James Allen

Once back at the hotel, I spent the evening reviewing what I might say. I had never spoken to such a large group, and I felt a tremendous responsibility. I thought back to the Indian who said a gratitude prayer for the rain, so I knelt down and followed the same pattern. I thanked the Lord for the opportunity to be speaking at such an event, for loosening my tongue to say beneficial words of inspiration, and that my mind was clear and peaceful. I envisioned it going wonderfully and beyond my highest expectations.

The next morning, just before my turn to speak, I was sitting in the green room where I could hear the roaring crowd. There were fifteen thousand people in the room with another five thousand in an adjoining conference room watching live on a mega screen. The energy was electric, and I was excited and grateful for the opportunity. I prayed fervently to be guided in my words, that I might say what the Lord would have me say.

My name was announced and a thunderous applause shook the stage.

{A portion of my talk about "When It Comes to Money Matters"}

"I'm grateful for the opportunity to be with you all this morning. Your energy is contagious, and I've come to learn about the good you all are doing in the world, and I am genuinely impressed.

"Let me see if I have this right. At some point, you decided that you wanted more out of life. You decided perhaps to be

your own boss, become an entrepreneur, and break the chain of generational financial scarcity. I can definitely relate.

"About ten years ago, I married my high school sweetheart, and early in our marriage we decided we wanted to be entrepreneurs. Unfortunately, we couldn't even spell entrepreneur. Growing up, money was never really discussed in our homes, because it was often a sore subject. I remember the day of my wedding just like it was yesterday. My former step-father opened his wallet and pulled out a twenty-dollar bill. He gave it to me. I know it doesn't sound like much, but it was a special moment between us. To date, he had never given me cash like that before. But it was my wedding, so it made sense on this special occasion.

"As he handed me the money, these unforgettable words left his lips: 'Here you go son, and don't worry—you can pay me back when you get it. I know times will be tough as you are starting out.' Friends, this was not a wedding gift, this was a loan! Now you all should know that I just paid that deal off last week, so things are good."

(Laughter erupted from the crowd)

"You know what baffled me the most about that whole situation? It wasn't that he had asked me to pay him back that measly amount of money. It was the complete surety and belief that my step-father knew and declared that starting out, times <u>would be</u> tough. So one day I decided to question his limiting belief. This caused me to question other beliefs I had been told my whole life, especially when it came to money. Why? Because, if I didn't want to follow in the path of those who had very little financial abundance, I knew I had to question their language and their stinkin' thinkin'.

"You see, we go through life taking on common beliefs

that sometimes just aren't true, and it can be damaging to our ability to create, especially when it comes to wealth.

"For example, finish this sentence for me: Rules are meant to be . . ."

(The large crowd yelled out in confidence, "Broken!" I stood silently staring at the audience with a skeptical look on my face.)

"Hmm, I'm curious to know who taught you that? Who here has teenagers who are driving? Raise your hands. All right; let's apply this. You hand your child the car keys and say, 'Son or daughter, today rules are meant to be broken! Go as fast as you want, and wherever you want!'

"I do not know a parent on the planet who would honestly say that to their child. Yet somewhere along the line we were taught that in order to get ahead or to make it big you have to break the rules.

"So let me take the opportunity to give you the correct answer. **Rules are meant to be FOLLOWED.** *Success leaves clues. Those who have earned a spot at the top of this organization have done so because they've followed the rules and habits that will reward anyone who decides to do the same.*

"Here's an immediate rule to follow: **Copy what great achievers do, and you'll get what they get.** *Significant accomplishments are no respecter of persons. They compensate anyone who follows the rules and success patterns. I am witness that this rule works.*

"Several years ago, I decided to get into the financial services industry. I remember my interview with the gentleman who was considering hiring me. I asked him, 'Are

there high six and seven figure earners in this company?'

"He replied, 'Of course there are.'

"'What are their names?' I asked.

"He began to freely tell me a few names, and I took out a piece of paper and began to write them down.

"'Why are you writing down their names?' he questioned.

"'For two reasons, sir. One, I know if it's been done it can be done. I know that if there are people who have hit the mark, I can hit the mark too.'

"'And what's the second reason?' he wondered.

"'The second reason is that I know people are going to come along, especially people close to me, family and friends, and they are going to say things like, 'Oh be careful of that industry!' or 'That deal doesn't work; we've tried it or we know someone who's tried it.' Then I can pull out my little piece of paper with the people who are doing it and say, 'Yes it does work, and here are the names to prove it!'

"I knew I would have to guard my environment from nay-sayers. In fact, if someone ever gives me advice that is going to detract from my goals and dreams, I say, 'What is your address?' They always ask why, of course, and the answer is, 'So I can forward my bills to you for your advice!'

(The audience laughed with amusement.)

"It's great! Negative dream killers stopped giving me advice and were dispelled from my environment. This is another rule to follow, my friends: **You must control your environment and your sphere of influence.** There should be a sign on your personal door that says, **Only positive contributors welcome here!"**

(An unexpected uproar of cheering broke out in the audience)

"I believe what Ralph Waldo Emerson said when he quipped, 'You become an average of the five people you decide to hang around most in life.' Recently I heard another powerful insight of this truth by a wise grandmother. She said, 'Show me your friends, and I will show you your future.'

*This not only refers to who you surround yourself with, but it also heavily refers to what you surround yourself with. What books do you read? What movies or shows do you watch? And what do you spend your time looking at on your phone? Is it productive? Is it propelling you toward your goals and dreams? If not, eliminate it! Clean up your environment, because **distractions equal destruction**.*

"There are plenty of mind-numbing temptations that are looking to rob you of your full potential. If it's not a contributor, it's a potential detractor, and successful people in any endeavor have figured out how to filter out and eliminate distractions.

"You know what? I just had an impression, so I am going to act on it. Everyone within the sound of my voice, write down at least three things in your environment that are not serving you— three things you know you should eliminate from your life that are not contributing to your highest good. Go ahead. Do it! This is personal, and I imagine some of you have some big things you need to let go of, so please respect your fellow team members around you by focusing on your own distractions. Or as the Bible says, focus on the beam in your own eye.

(I let the room fall soberly silent as the large audience took to their notepads with a humble realization that we all have things we can eliminate from our lives.)

Three Distractions to Eliminate:

1. _____

_____

2. _____

_____

3. _____

_____

"Now that you have created space in your life by eliminating some things that are not serving you, write down at least three actions you know you should be doing specifically to succeed. Three is the minimum, not the maximum, so if you think of more, jot them down.

"Maybe some of you just need to be reading a lot more good books written by high achievers. Maybe you need to take time to simply follow up more often, with more people, to get the deal done. This is a huge rule to follow.

*"Actually, let me just put some weight on that. **The fortune, my friends, is in the follow up**. I'm bold enough to say that **this game of business, regardless of the specific industry, is flat-out won or lost in your ability to follow up.** You may have a superior product or service, but the prize will go to the person who decides to follow up the most."*

(I stopped talking for a minute and let them write down their commitments.)

Three Actions to Implement for Success:

1. _____

_____

2. _____

_____

3. _____

_____

"Okay, let's get back to the story. You should know that I boldly wrote my name on that piece of paper along with the other high earners, because I also know another rule to follow that ensures success. **We have to first see ourselves being successful in our minds, and we have to speak like we are already achieving it before it can come to fruition. You must imagine it in your mind as reality first, then comes the accomplishment.**

"All things, good or bad, start with an idea or a thought. Then we start bringing it to pass when we begin talking about it. Our language propels us to action—good or bad, what you want or what you don't want. Either way, your physical environment knows no different. It sets out to achieve what you think and talk about. My good friend, mindset expert David Bayer, teaches, **'Our brain is a goal achieving machine.'**

"Guess what? The path was not easy for me, and I almost gave up. I had to take a life insurance exam. It was a *hundred-question test, and I didn't pass the first time. So, I took it again, and I didn't pass a second time. So I took it a third time; by this point I was on a first name basis at the testing center, and I didn't pass the third time. Then it happened. People who were close to me started expressing things like, 'We told you so' and 'This is a sign that you should do something else.'*

"Well, I could have listened to them, but gratefully I surrounded myself with positive contributors, such as books from Zig Ziglar, who said, **'Obstacles are those things we see when we take our eyes off the goal.'** *The goal was not to pass the test. The goal was to be added to the list of high achievers. So, I took that test a fourth, and I didn't pass again. This is getting exciting, isn't it?*

"*Now, there is a popular saying here in Las Vegas, and it goes, 'Fifth time's a charm.' This proved true for me, because I nailed that test on the fifth time. You had to score at least a 70 percent to pass, and I scored a 70 percent straight up.*

"*I went back to the gentleman who hired me, excited that I had finally passed. I was thinking,* Finally, I can get started writing business. *However, he said there were actually three more tests I had to take and pass. To make a long story short, of the four tests I had to take and pass, I only took them twelve times. You heard that right—twelve times! Now I was thinking about this just the other day. I am a pretty competitive guy, and no one has beaten my record yet.*"

(A hearty laugh came from the group, perhaps relating to my life perspective.)

"*You see, I'm always winning at something. I'm always going to find some victory in the battle. Let me put it this way, and this is an extremely important muscle for you to develop* and exercise, especially as an entrepreneur. **You must be able to identify and celebrate the victories, regardless of the score.** Focus on what you did right or what you did great. It might be that you just got back up after being knocked down. Perhaps it is recognizing a mistake and learning from it. Or maybe you decided to make another phone call after a top prospect told you no. Whatever it is, look for it, and celebrate it!

"Well, believe it or not, success did not come instantaneously just because I had my licenses. It doesn't work like that. Work, effort, and grit are always required. Thomas Edison expressed it best when he said, **'Most people miss opportunity, because it shows up in a pair of overalls and looks like work.'**

"For two years I worked and struggled to make it in that industry. Because it was straight commission, I had to find other jobs that would bring in cash flow consistently to support my family. There came a point when I was working three other jobs in addition to financial services. I was doing valet parking, teaching tennis lessons, and working at a cold-calling sales center at night. Then came the test. I'd been at it for two years, and a particularly challenging month passed where I only made $87 from financial services. I figured I had given it a good fight, and it was time for me to throw in the towel and quit. I went to the gentleman who hired me and said, 'I just don't think this is for me.'

"Then he said something that made me reconsider. He said, **'Thomas, the only way you fail is if you quit.'**

"Now why did he have to go and say something like that to a guy like me? He knew I was competitive, and he knew that would stir me up. Which it did! So I made a decision—really, *my wife and I made a decision to go for it! To really go for it and burn the ships behind us with no opportunity for retreat. We realized we hadn't FULLY DECIDED yet.*

"Ralph Waldo Emerson was spot on when he said, **'When a decision is made, the universe conspires to make it happen.'**

"Another key factor was I wanted to play at the top level, and the people I was copying in my office were not playing at the top level. So I sought out one of the leaders whose name was on my little paper. I found out where he lived and operated his business. This was before GPS, so I had to make some phone calls, and cross some boundaries that some might not be willing to cross.

"I drove eight hours to see this man, found him, and said 'Congratulations, you're my new mentor!'

"He said, 'Who are you?'

"I said, 'Exactly the problem! You don't know who I am, and I'm a somebody. I'm going to do what you do and say what you say.'

"He told me, 'But I don't train or mentor anyone who is not in my organization.'

"To which I replied, 'Until today, because I made a decision to go for it, and you are one of the people making it happen in a big way!'

"When he realized I was not leaving and I was serious, he agreed to mentor and coach me, but I would have to pay for it. He presented the amount required. I could either see it as a payment or as an investment. And by the way, he only gave me about a minute to decide. I already knew the return I would get

by copying this successful leader, and now I just had to make the investment. I simply said, 'Yes!'

"It's important to understand that he was not trying to sell me on his mentorship. Rather, he presented something of value, and I had to decide if I was willing to invest to get the return. **I've learned that a person of wealth and abundance is not sold anything; rather, once they see value, they invest in it.**

"Can I tell you the result of making a decision and copying a successful mentor? Do you remember the month before when I made $87? Remember? Well, the next four months we went full-time in financial services and made $124,000! Some might say our situation changed overnight. It certainly felt that way. However, let me remind you that we struggled for more than two years, and I almost quit.

"Thomas Edison put it this way: **'Many of life's failures are people who did not realize how close they were to success when they gave up.'**

"From that point, as a team, we doubled our income a few times and built a successful agency with more than one hundred agents in three different locations."

(The lively organization wanted to cheer for the accomplishment, but I broke it up by continuing.)

"Finish this sentence: 'Money doesn't grow on . . .'

(Again, they all answered with sureness, "Trees!")

"Hmm, really? Then you've obviously never met a farmer with an apple or citrus farm or one that grows and sells nuts. All their money grows on trees, and I've met some pretty wealthy tree farmers. Perhaps many of the things we've been *taught, or that society believes, just aren't true.*

"What if the how-to-see-the-world lenses you were prescribed from your upbringing and environment have limited your vision?

"Dr. Wayne Dyer said it brilliantly: **'When you change the way you look at things, the things you look at change.'**

"It's not that anyone at the top of this organization is any better than those who are not. It's simply that at some point **they saw and believed things differently, made a decision, and copied someone who was already doing it.** *That's the formula my friends.*

"Now, by a show of hands, how many of you joined this company and opportunity because of the money potential?"

(From what I could see, about half of the hands were raised.)

"Okay, how many of you joined because you wanted to run your own business and be your own boss?"

(Many of the same hands went up.)

"I see some of you haven't raised your hands yet so let me ask. How many of you actually don't know why you're here—it's just that someone said Las Vegas *and you said you were in?"*

(A surge of laughter broke out, and many jovial hands flung in the air.)

"Let's actually talk about the money for a moment. We all tend to do things for different reasons, and that is perfectly all right. Money tends to be a motivating factor.

"*However, a wise religious leader, Thomas Monson, once said, '***People will work hard for money, but they'll work harder for another person. And they'll work hardest of all for a cause they believe in.***'*

"*I realize that making money is definitely important. It facilitates so much in this world. I also know if you will attach whatever you do to make money to a cause, you will have a lot more of it, and it won't even feel like work.*

"*Maybe the cause is earning enough to retire a parent or grandparent. Maybe it is getting out of debt. Maybe it is paying cash for a dream vacation. Maybe it is taking your parents on a dream vacation. Maybe you have a philanthropic heart, and you want to support a cause in another country. All of these examples require money, and in some cases a lot of it.*

"*When my wife, Kimberly, was a teenager she promised herself that one day she would take her parents on an all-expense-paid vacation to Hawaii. This desire was instilled in her because her parents had always wanted to go and had even saved for several years to go with some of her mom's siblings. However, when the time came, her father was struck with cancer, and all their funds saved for Hawaii were used to pay for doctor bills.*

"*When we got married, Kimberly told me about this dream, and we set out to accomplish it. Well, four years ago we made that dream a reality for my in-laws. We even hired a professional photographer to capture their special moment.*

(I showed a picture on the big screen of them in love, holding hands on the beach in Maui. A spontaneous applause broke out in the crowd.)

"I'm so glad we had those pictures taken, because little did we know that it would not be long before my beloved father-in-law would pass away. You can imagine how much we all treasure these photos now.

"Remember, my friends, you'll work the hardest of all for a cause you believe in.

"Take a moment and write down three causes that ring true to you.

(Again, I stopped talking for a minute and let them write down their three causes.)

Your Three Causes:

1. _____

   _____

2. _____

   _____

3. _____

   _____

"As I mentioned before, whatever your driving factor is, money is typically required to fund it, and I want to help facilitate your ability to attract more of it.

"First, your language. The very words that cross your lips have to give money a green light to flow into your life. So, you have to eliminate words that are giving it a red light. Remember this. **You cannot attract that which you criticize.**

"You must find yourself saying a lot more of **'I can afford that!'** and **'How can I afford that?'** Instead of 'I can't afford that' or 'That's too expensive.' The moment you say you can't, or that it's too expensive, all possibilities are destroyed. I'm certainly not suggesting you run out and purchase something on credit that is frivolous or unnecessary. I am suggesting, however, that if you want to buy something, make it a goal to earn the money to pay for it.

"Recently, my wife and I were at the doctor and I couldn't believe my ears when the nurse commented, 'I am broke, I've always been broke, I'll die broke, and I'm good with *that.' I was tempted to ask him, 'Do you really want to be broke, or have you just become complacent?'* **A simple language adjustment would change that money rejection into wealth attraction.** *We will always bring about what we talk about, so always speak in terms that all things are possible and even such things as, 'I am a money magnet!'*

*"Go ahead say it out loud: '**I am a money magnet!**'"*

(The crowd blurted out with conviction, "I am a money magnet!")

"That sounded good, and it should feel good, too. If you were hesitant to say it, the money will hesitate to show up. That's why it's important to say things that attract money often, because it will help dispel any abundance road blocks."

(Without warning a small group in the crowd yelled out again, "I am a money magnet!" It caught like a wild fire, and others throughout the arena joined in.)

"I love it! Now, just because someone makes a lot of money doesn't mean they have a lot of money, or even know how to manage it. We often see this with professional athletes who are drafted and become instant millionaires and who, up to that point, might have experienced a financially impoverished childhood. The stats on bankruptcy among professional athletes are staggering. The incredible reality is, in an industry like yours, one can experience an enormous amount of financial success and still be broke.

(I raised one eyebrow and started in with a skeptical tone.)

"Finish this sentence . . ."

(The crowd broke into laughter from my previous play on these exercises.)

"No, really, I think you'll get this one right: 'It's not how much you make, it's how much you . . .'"

(About 50 percent of the audience responded, "Keep!")

"That's right, it's how much you keep. Interesting enough, I've met people who earn six and sometimes seven figures and who are three months away from disaster. In contrast, I've met a school teacher and part-time football coach and a firefighter who are earning well below six figures that could live for two years or more and be financially okay without another paycheck. Who do you think lives a happier, more peaceful life?

"Would you all be okay if I shared with you a wealth system that when followed will ensure you accumulate wealth and never have money problems? Here it is. Write this down.

{Power Paragraphs}

{"There is a pattern among the wealthy regardless of their background, race, religion, ethnicity, or age. It is simply how they manage their income. They live by a wealth system I call the 10/10/10/70 rule. Once you receive income, just follow this rule and everything will work out. These numbers represent a percentage of your income and who you pay first.

"I've learned people of good fortune are giving people, whether it be to their church, a charity, or a cause they believe in. They believe in the givers gain method, or what the Bible calls the law of tithing. So, the very first 10 percent is given away to a higher cause. The promise in the last book the Old Testament says that when you give 10 percent to a righteous cause, the Lord will open the windows of heaven and pour out

a blessing that there will not be room enough to receive it. The first 10 percent, then, is given away to a higher cause.

"I learned this law when I was a mere seven years old. My grandfather, Glenn Smith, in his wisdom set out to teach me this valuable lesson. He had several pecan trees in his yard, and he contracted me to pick the pecans up off the ground and put them into large paper grocery bags. For every bag I filled I got a whopping one-dollar bill. To a seven-year-old, that was some serious dinero back then. So, I went to work feverishly filling up those bags with pecans. It took quite a bit of work to fill the big bags with those little pecans. My goal was to fill ten bags, and by the end of the day I had done it. I remember just like it was yesterday, I had lined up the ten bags on the back patio in a perfectly straight line for my grandfather to see. Then came the reward, an amount of money I had never held in my hands up to that point. He placed each dollar bill individually in my hands, counting them one by one. My eyes grew larger and larger with each additional dollar. I was a little confused when he stopped at nine dollars, though, and I thought for sure he had miscounted. So I reminded him that there were ten bags, which would merit ten dollars.

"Then he pulled out an envelope and said, "One of your dollars is in this envelope, so you can contribute 10 percent to tithing."

"At first I was devastated. A whole dollar, *I thought.* Does he realize how long it took me to just fill up one bag with pecans?

"Then, sensing my disappointment, my dear grandfather took me outside and showed me the big beautiful pecan trees that God had provided, and he reminded me how blessed we were to only have to give back 10 percent and how

we get to keep 90 percent. I remember him tenderly telling me about the promised blessings in the Bible in his own words: 'Everything will always work out, Tommy, if you pay the Lord first.' I have never forgotten that lesson, and I have always given the first 10 percent of everything I've earned from that day forward.

"The next 10 percent is called a 'You Fund.' I also call this a 'Grateful Savings Fund.'

"Here's what that means. You are Grateful you had some extra money just in case an unexpected expense arrives. Some might call it an emergency fund, but I choose to call it our grateful savings fund, because I am always grateful I have it when I need it. It is NOT a vacation fund or for buying a big-screen T.V.

"Most people would sleep a lot better, and be nicer to their spouses if they had $15,000 to $20,000 dollars just sitting in their savings account. So remember, the second 10 percent is the 'YOU Fund' or 'Grateful Savings Fund.'

"The next 10 percent is what I call a 'Future Fund.' These funds are allocated to some sort of higher-interest-bearing account that you can use for retirement, or at least the option to continue working because you want to, not because you have to. This third 10 percent is for the future.

"Finally, the last 70 percent is used for everything else. Home payment, expenses, debt payments, food, entertainment, you name it. Issues come because many people's 70 percent is 100 percent, or they spend 100 percent and sometimes more of their income. So when an emergency does show up, their only retreat is to borrow from a credit card, which can be a scary cycle.

"If you want to buy something like a new entertainment center, for example, then save up for it by starting an entertainment center fund. Just remember that it must be from the 70 percent section.

(I put a picture up on the big screen that showed the numbers vertically.)

"Keeping it simple, let's say you brought home $8,000 a month. Your wealth system would look like this:

10%: $800—Tithing or Charitable Cause

10%: $800—You Fund (Grateful Savings Fund), $9,600 in 12 months!

10%: $800—Future Fund, $328,826 in 20 years at 5% compounded interest!

70%: $5,600 — Everything else

"Another key factor is to make the top portion or the 10/10/10 as automatic as possible. For example, if you know how much comes in every month, you can set up an automatic transfer from your checking into your savings and future accounts. If your income varies every month, set up an automatic withdrawal for the amount you know at minimum you are going to earn, then manually transfer the rest the day you get paid.

"Going forward it should be easy to know if you can pay for something or not. If you have extra money in the 70 percent category, then you know you can buy it. Also, you must come to a realization that if you want more and don't have the money, then you must earn more. You should also know that the wealthy are constantly increasing the top portions and decreasing the bottom portion to look something more like 15/20/20/45. They get more excited about giving and saving

than spending, which I believe attracts more. For many of you, this represents a big shift in thinking."}

(I paused momentarily to let the process sink in.)

"What a blessing and good fortune you all have to be part of an organization that allows you to earn an unlimited amount, and in turn keep an unlimited amount. Some say, 'I'm not paid what I'm worth,' and this might be true, because they have no potential to earn more in their current set of circumstances. But that is not the case for you. You will make what you are worth, and the great thing is, you are the one who determines your value. No one else. If you want things to get better, then YOU have to get better. If you want to earn more, then YOU personally have to become more valuable. The great Jim Rohn says it best:

'If you want to make a living work at a job, but if you want to make a fortune, work on yourself.'

"You have to be willing to see things differently, speak as if anything is possible, and DECIDE to really go for it like you never have before!

"Let this be your day of decision, my friends, and may you be blessed in your efforts.

"Thank you."

(The arena erupted with a standing ovation, and I was humbled and overcome with gratitude that the message seemed to arrive at their hearts.)

Back in the green room, the thrill of speaking to such a large, enthusiastic crowd washed over me. My mind drifted back to having a fairly successful business. The transition from financial services to seeking out a vocation in speaking came in part because I had been asked to speak two or three times a month by other organizations that had heard of my success story. Eventually, enough people told me it was a path I should pursue, so I began stepping away from financial services and seeking out a vocation that I didn't even know was an option. Truthfully, it found me. When I came across the speech contest, I figured it was a great way to kick it off. Little did I know that it would turn into this incredible movement.

I offered a silent prayer and thanked the Lord for guiding my words, and for giving me the opportunity.

I stayed and enjoyed some of the other speakers who followed me then I asked one of the security staff to accompany me to my hotel room to make sure there were no fake chauffeur's looming in the wings. Once back in my room, I had a little time before I needed to head to the airport, so I took out the book and began to write.

The wealth system and principles I just spoke about are true. I have taught them to countless numbers of people. More importantly, I know of their verity because I have lived by them.

Whether you make a little or a lot, if you speak with the language of abundance and live by the wealth system, you'll always have enough and to spare. You may have to do some serious lifestyle adjusting, but I promise you'll sleep better and you'll find life is more peaceful. When you are giving to a righteous cause, have a grateful fund, and are putting money toward your future, everything else seems to fall into place.

Chapter 11

The Language of Those Who Win

As I made my way out of that elegant Las Vegas Hotel, some attendees from the conference recognized me as one of the speakers and rushed over to greet me. I was humbled that they had taken some inspiration from my talk, and I wished them well as I attempted to catch my ride to the airport. Then all of a sudden, many others from the conference had joined them in a large circle around me. Many of their phones were already out and now recording me. So in a formal, authoritative manner, I said the first thing that came to mind: "I bet you are all wondering why I called this meeting here today?" A string of laughter ignited the small crowd. "Remember, all of this will be for naught unless you put it into action. I'll leave you all with this. I love something W. Clement Stone said about taking action:

"I think there is something, more important than believing: Action! The world is full of dreamers; there aren't enough who will move ahead and begin to take concrete steps to actualize their vision."

"So go forward and speak into existence that which you really want. Then take the necessary actions!" I held up my hand and counted to three with my fingers, saying, **Say, Do, Achieve!** Best wishes to you all, my friends."

They gave me a farewell applause and I made my way for the door. One of them shouted out, "Rules are meant to be followed!" Another took confidence and yelled, "Money does grow on trees!" I looked back and pointed in their direction with a smile. "That's right, I love that perspective!"

Fortunately, my driver looked like my real driver, and I did not feel any anxiety. I was, however, constantly on guard for any suspicious people. I kept the book and Dr. Wright's notes in my computer bag that was almost always either on my shoulder or locked in the safe in my hotel room. While in the back seat of the executive car, I pulled out my phone to check on my flight. I noticed Clem had been trying to call, so I dialed him back.

"Hi, Clem, sorry I missed your call. It was a little crazy getting out of the hotel."

"Is everything okay?" he anxiously asked.

"Yes, I'm actually on my way to the airport and everyone seems to be in good standing if you know what I mean," I said as I peered at the chauffeur.

"Okay, I made arrangements for you to meet someone while you were in Las Vegas," Clem explained.

"All right, I'll need to push back my flight then."

"No worries, our travel folks have already made arrangements for you to fly out later this evening. I am going to text you the address of the café where you will meet him in one hour."

"Great, who am I meeting at the café?" I asked.

"His name is Daniel Ruettiger, and he has your picture. So don't worry, he will find you."

"All right, anything else I need to know, Clem?"

"That's it for now; we'll be in touch," he said and bid me farewell.

I notified my driver that there had been a change of plans, and asked if he would take me to the address Clem had just texted me. I gathered all my luggage and took it with me into the café. It was a small mom-and-pop shop on the southwest end of the city that had been around for at least twenty-five years. I found a seat and explained I was waiting for someone who was coming in about forty-five minutes, so I would just take a glass of water with a lemon for now.

I thought I would take advantage of the time, so I pulled out the book and began to review the final page of notes, page 8.

The Language of Those Who Win

Among those who consistently win in their lives resides a positive dialect of certainty and confidence that whatever they set out to do will result in a victory. They have figured out the power of self-mastery; and are champions of mental toughness. They approach any feat with an "I Can Do It" and "I Will Do It" attitude. They speak in terms of never giving up, always putting in the necessary effort, and always rising after they fall.

Winners are clear that one word separates amateurs from professionals in any industry, any athletic competition, or any of life's roles. The word is FOCUS. The professional obtains the discipline to focus a little longer in the moment of battle or in preparing for the battle, and that makes all the difference.

After reading Dr. Wright's notes, I glanced over at a wall in the café that was filled with framed pictures and noticed this was no ordinary place. There were several autographed photographs of famous athletes, actors, and business icons who had apparently graced this modest café. One picture in particular stood out to me. It was of swimming legend, Michael Phelps. In the picture, he was draped with several gold medals: with his hands on his hips, he had an eagle-eye focus.

I took out the book and began to write.

Imagine lining up at the starting blocks next to Michael Phelps at the Olympics. What do you think Michael's language is when compared to those who are competing to knock him from his throne? I am sure his language is full of words such as, "I got this," "I own this," and "Stay focused." He gets in the winning zone and adheres to no other distractions. Meanwhile, those competing against him are thinking the same thing, perhaps, but with an undertone of doubt such as, "I hope to do my best," "I'll try to win," and "I think I can win." Obviously the results don't lie—we see that Michael Phelps was definitely more certain than the others that he was going to win.

I closed the book, secured it under my right arm like a football, and walked over to the wall of fame to get a closer look at the pictures and personal messages. One in particular intrigued me; it was of the stoically motivational sports movie *Rudy*. It showed the movie cover, and in the corner was a picture of the real Rudy, whose life was portrayed in the movie. He had penned a simple message and signed the photo, "Always do more doing than thinking!" That made sense to me, and just like everything, I'm sure there was a story behind it.

Just then a gentleman behind me interrupted my train of thought. "I need to give them another picture. That one makes me look mean, and I really am a nice guy." A thrill went up my spine as I turned around and was face to face with the guy in the picture—the real Rudy. I was speechless.

"Are you Thomas?" He knew my name; what was going on?

Then it dawned on me that this was the guy I was supposed to meet. Daniel Ruettiger was "Rudy."

"Hi! Pleasure to meet you. Yes, I am Thomas."

"How about we sit down and chat?" Rudy said.

I started in. "Let me just say that your story is amazing. I've seen the movie several times, and I'm inspired every time."

"Yeah, all I did was make a tackle, and they made a movie out of it. It was no big deal," he coaxed with sarcasm. "Tell me about you, Mr. Thomas, what's great in your life?"

"Well, I'm married to my high school sweetheart. We have been blessed with four beautiful girls, and we currently live in Virginia," I responded.

"I hear you are quite the speaker?" He prodded.

"Well, I won a speech contest, and now I'm writing a book about it. It's no big deal," I mused with the same flair of sarcasm.

"Ha ha, I like that. So, what questions do you have for me?" Rudy asked.

"Thank you kindly for meeting with me. Right now, I'm writing about the language of those who win. Any insights on that?" I inquired.

Rudy took in a deep breath and looked over to his picture on the wall. "Did you see what I wrote on that picture over there?"

"Yes. I read it, and I was curious to know what prompted you to write it," I responded.

"Well, had I thought of everything I was going to have to do to get accepted into Notre Dame, I would never have done it! I just thought, I want to go to Notre Dame, so I am going to do what it takes to get in. Then, once I got in—after four attempts mind you—I had this incredible notion that I wanted to play on the football team of the Fighting Irish. I wasn't big enough. I wasn't strong enough. Nor was I athletic enough. Nonetheless, I wanted to be on the team. So I just went forward and did it. Now, had I thought of all the reasons why I couldn't do it, or the mere fact that I might realistically get killed, I would never have done it!"

His voice was raised now in excitement as he continued to explain his story. "So, Thomas, the point is, **always do more doing than thinking!** Many people think themselves right out of what they really want, instead of getting started and plunging forward!"

"Wow . . . that is so spot-on, Rudy," I reinforced.

"And I'll tell you, that making the movie was a whole other Rudy story in and of itself. Seriously! If I would have thought of everything that went into making a movie, I would never have done it. I thought it was a good inspirational story, but no one else seemed to think so. For ten years, no producers would entertain my story. Then one day, the same Hollywood producer who made the movie *Hoosiers* said he would take a look at it. He told me to meet him at a café in Hollywood and we would discuss it. So I flew out to California on a limited budget and showed up to the café, but the producer never showed up."

"Wow, so what did you do?" I inquired

"Here was another one of those moments to do more doing than thinking. I started asking people in the restaurant if they knew this fellow I was supposed to meet, and I finally met a guy who said he did! So I asked him if he knew where the producer lived. He said he did. So I asked him if he'd be willing to take me to his house. He said he would. I went and knocked on the producer's door, but he was not there. So I decided I was going to sit on his door step until he showed up. I stayed there quite a long time, a longer time than most would have been willing to stay. Then finally, the producer showed up, and I walked right up to him, extended my hand and said, 'I'm Rudy, and you're late!' The producer was apologetic and was impressed that I would find out where he lived and not move until he came home."

The producer said, 'You're the real deal aren't you? This isn't just some story, is it? You live this way. I'm going to take a good hard look at your script.'

"And there you have it. He produced the movie. Had I not gone to that extreme, there may have never been a *Rudy* movie. Now I don't tell many people this, Thomas, but four United States presidents have personally invited me to watch the movie in the White House theatre. So I think it has had a bit of an impact."

"That is incredible! Thank you for sharing that with me. I get it now," I confirmed.

Rudy jumped in again, "You know, Thomas, there are so many other stories in the making of the movie that almost shut the whole thing down, but fortunately we just kept moving forward. Many doors were closed on us, but I don't think we have time to discuss all of them."

"You've been so generous to me with your time; thank you, Rudy. Do you mind if we take a picture together?"

"Not at all—just take the picture, don't out-think it!" he responded jokingly.

Rudy and me at the café

Once on the airplane heading back to the east coast, I wanted to get some sleep, but the one-year period marking when I would have to finish the book and report back at the hotel in Boston was closing in fast. So I turned on the light over my seat and began to write.

What Rudy said about "doing more doing than thinking" is definitely true. I remember as a freshman tennis player in high school, I had an experience where I did more doing than thinking.

My doubles partner, who was a junior, had never been to the state tournament, and all we had to do was get to the finals of the regional tournament to be selected to go to state. Without knowing any different, I told my doubles partner, "We are going to state; we just have to win the next match in the semi-finals and we are in." I could sense his hesitation, but I didn't pay much attention to it. We got in the zone and played our best tennis. We won the first set 6–4, then something interesting happened. People started gathering around and taking interest in our match.

One of the opposing players was so distraught at losing the first set that he busted one of his rackets against the net pole. It's a good thing a referee didn't see it, or he would have been disqualified. We went back and forth in the second set and ended up pulling it off, winning 6–4, 6–4. There was a lot of cheering from people I didn't even know, which was not a typical thing in our high school matches. We shook our opponent's hands, and then I turned to my doubles partner, who was visibly emotional about the whole thing.

I said, "It's no big deal, partner, we're just going to the state tournament."

When he finally gathered his composure he said, "No, you don't understand. Not only are we going to state, we just beat the defending state champions! We've knocked them completely out of the state tournament!"

It took me a moment to take in what he just told me, and it made sense now why the other team was getting so heated and why the spectators were getting so excited. Somehow, I missed the memo that we were playing the defending state champions. Maybe someone told me, but I must have blocked it out and just focused on getting to state regardless of who or what was in our path. Essentially, I did more doing than thinking because I could have easily out-thought myself in that situation.

At the state tournament, my partner and I made it to the third round, ultimately losing to the team that won it all. We were the only ones to win a set against them, though.

The language of those that win leaves no room for doubt or hesitation. They are never out of the game, regardless of the score.

Satisfied with my most recent contributions, I closed the treasured leather-bound notebook, turned out my seat light, and slept the rest of the flight.

Back home, autumn was in the air, and the lush green foliage was turning brilliant colors. One of our family's favorite things to do in the fall is to have a leaf-raking day that consists of me doing most of the raking while the girls jump in my piles. Someone once said, and it makes more sense to me now, **'Cherish the small things, because one day they will become the big things.'**

A few weeks later, Clem let me know I had one more place to go before we'd meet in Boston. He and his father were able to get me into an elite conference, for which participants had to qualify. They weren't sure who the guest speaker was going to be, but the organization always brought in someone who had won big in their life.

I flew to San Antonio, Texas and made my way to the hotel on the famed River Walk where the conference was to be held. I met a gal at the door to the small conference room who was making sure no unauthorized people entered. "Hello, Kathy, how's your beautiful day going?" I greeted her after reading her name badge.

"Well, it's going better now with that kind salutation," she responded with a smile. "And whom do I have the pleasure of meeting today?" she inquired.

"My name is Thomas Blackwell, and I was sent—"

Before I could even finish my thought she blurted out, "Oh, here you are, Mr. Blackwell! Put on your name badge and feel free to find a seat anywhere you like. Mr. Gable will be here shortly, and welcome to Tiger School."

I entered the small conference room with only about twenty-five seats and wondered exactly what "Tiger School" was. And, was Mr. Gable the speaker or the host? As seems to be his pattern, Clem didn't give me much background on the conference. I glanced around at the other attendees, who cordially nodded and smiled. We all greeted each other with just our body language until a gentleman approached the podium and began to speak.

"I want to congratulate you all for being selected to attend this year's Tiger School! With the insights you will glean, it is sure to be a monumental day in your lives. We hold this elite event every year for those who have accomplished something significant and are ready to take it to the next level. You all come from different backgrounds, but have something in common. You've learned how to win at some level. You've been selected by someone on the board of directors who are scattered throughout the whole world. They are able to select one person a year. So again, congratulations on being the one! Without further ado, I would like to introduce the man who will be speaking to you today. He is a true champion, an elite competitor, and a legend in the wrestling world."

The host continued, "As a competitor, Dan Gable was a three-time Iowa High School State Champion. He was a three-time Big Eight Champion at Iowa State University, a three-time All-American, and his college prep record was 182 wins and 1 loss. He was the 1971 World Champion and won the Gold Medal in the Munich 1972 Olympics without even surrendering a single point! He has been named one of the top 100 Olympians of all time. As a coach at the University of Iowa, he has led the Hawkeye wrestling team to 15 NCAA titles, 9 of which were consecutive, 21 Big Ten Team titles, and 7 perfect seasons. He has produced 45 individual National Champions, 152 All-Americans, 106 Big Ten Champions, and 12 Olympians. He is a three-time Olympic head coach where several Gold Medals were won. Okay, Dan is in the back motioning me to stop, so let's get him up here. Ladies and gentlemen, please welcome one of the best athletes in the world, Mr. Dan Gable!"

We all quickly rose to our feet and applauded as Dan walked from the back of the room to the front. All of us were ready to write down whatever he had to say. Although many of us were not familiar with the wrestling world, there stood before us a champion, a winner, and someone who knew the language of those that win. I took out my notepad and began to write.

{Highlights from Dan Gable's Elite Training, in his words.}

"Failure is not something you want to get used to. You have to have a will to succeed, a will to win, not a wish to win. I have a simple philosophy on the wrestling mat. I shoot, I score. You shoot, I score. Either way, I score, and I'd rather not have you score at all! Can you apply this in life? The economy is good, I win. The economy is bad, I win. Either way I win!

"When I was younger, in high school, practice would be-

gin at 7:00 a.m., but I wanted to start practicing at 5:30 a.m. None of the coaches were willing to show up that early, so I asked them to just give me a key to the gym. My classmates would often walk by and see me early in the gym and say things like, 'I wonder what he's doing?' or 'Why is he doing that?' I think they know now . . . Pretty soon, other teammates joined me at 5:30 a.m., while the coaches would still show up at 7:00 a.m. We raised the standard of work ethic, and as a result, we raised our ability to win.

"I decided to start hanging around people who didn't entertain the option of losing. If you were going to hang out with me, you had better step up your game. I would always visualize myself winning—always. It's never too late to win or go after a dream. The goals and dreams you have are typically stuff you've read in books and from the environment around you.

"The best coaches in sports, business, or life know their players very well. They know what gets them excited, and what buttons to push, to keep them going. They care about their players personally. I had one loss in college, and I decided it was going to change my life for the better. I cut out a picture of the guy who beat me, and I carried it around in my wallet for years to remind me to always stay focused long enough to get the job done. That one loss was contributed to a lack of focus on my part. The guy who beat me struggled big time after that, because he didn't have any other goals or dreams after a big victory. Sure, celebrate the victories in your life, then set out to achieve some more. **Life does not determine a champion; a champion determines life**. Your attitude will carry you a lot further than talent will"

(During Dan's talk, he shifted his weight from side to side like he was ready to take someone down at any time. He carried this old, worn-out paper-back book rolled up like a gym towel in his right hand that he would point in our direction on occasion.)

"People are always asking me how I think the way I do. Where did I get all these ideas or notions to become a champion? And then I realized one day that it was the things I put in my head. It's these books of winners that I read. This book in my hand I always have with me, because it is my favorite, and it helped me develop this winning mentality. It's called, The Heart of a Champion *by Bob Richards. Bob has become a friend of mine now. He was the first athlete to be on the front of a Wheaties box.*

"I'm glad I made a DECISION to WIN and be a champion early in my life. Stop thinking it would be nice to win or that you'd like to win. Decide to win at whatever you do!"

It all went so fast. We each shook Dan's death-grip hand and then it was over. Many debriefing thoughts raced through my head, so I retreated to my hotel room so I could write. I sat down at the desk and began.

There is no doubt that Dan Gable is in an elevated league of those who win at the highest level. His talk today was all about how we too can achieve that level, if we will decide to win and put in the necessary effort. Those reading this book can perhaps relate to his tenacity on some level. I am sure we have all gone for something in our lives, right?

As he related his experience about asking for the gym keys to start working out earlier, it reminded me that I had done something similar.

In seventh and eighth grade, my mom dropped me off at my school tennis courts around 7:00 a.m. on her way to work.

School didn't start until 8:45 a.m., and I could have taken the bus close by my house, but I wanted to get there early so I could hit a tennis ball against the backboard for an hour and a half before school started. The tennis backboard was right in the path of my fellow students heading to their classes, and I too would hear them say things such as, "Why is he doing that?" and "He's here every day; when is he going to take a break?" Their words only propelled me to want to practice more.

This diligent effort and focus eventually allowed me to achieve my goal of competing at the Division I level in college. Somewhere early in life, I learned that **when you do things others aren't willing to do, you'll achieve things others won't.**

The language of those who win involves more than just the will. One must speak, think, and act in terms of winning. Unfortunately, on occasion one can have the desire and the talent, but if his language is not congruent it is highly unlikely that victory will ensue. Remember, **winners say they CAN, and losers say they can't.**

Our environment and belief system play enormous roles in our ability to win. If our surroundings are not conducive to winning all that is desired, that environment can be changed with a decision and a shift in our language.

A few years ago, before we moved to the east coast, I was asked by a high school basketball coach in southeast Arizona to come and speak to his team before the season started. The coach felt like he had compiled a very talented team that could go all the way, but there was a huge obstacle. For years, many in the little town believed that since the state had let private schools into their athletic division, it was nearly impossible for a small public school to win a state championship. Their debilitating complaint was, "You can make it to the playoffs, but then you'll have to face a private school and they are just too good." They even had solid evidence of why they would lose. Private schools could recruit anyone in the state, and the athletes often went on to play at major universities, while the small towns were only allowed to draw on the students in their respective districts. Thus the belief and language of an "unfair advantage" began to plague this small town and others that decided to adopt it. Before private schools were admitted, this particular high school had always competed well, and its teams had even won several state championships in a number of sports.

The coach was faced with a dilemma. He knew he had the talent on the team, but the players and the townspeople had to change their perspectives if things were going to change.

I remember it well. I met with the whole basketball team in one of their school conference rooms. There were about fifteen boys sitting in front of me in a horseshoe formation. I started out with my story, "Changing our Perspective". It was the same story I told to win the speech contest. It was especially fitting on this occasion, because this was the actual small town where Simpson saved my brother's life. I was born here, and I had spent several years of my youth in this area. We moved away when I was seven so my mother could pursue more schooling after my father passed away, but we still had a lot of family in this area.

I asked each boy what he wanted to accomplish this season. I started at the front right-hand side of the room and worked my way around the horseshoe.

The first boy, an experienced varsity player, said, "I want to make it to the playoffs."

The next boy fired off, "I want to have more baskets, rebounds, and assists than I did last year."

Another boy said he "just" wanted to beat their neighboring rival school. One after the other, similar responses were expressed, yet no one mentioned anything about being state champions, which would have been the highest achievement they could obtain.

Until the final young man seated on the left-hand side of the horseshoe, that is. A freshman, who had just moved to this small town, and who had been invited to the varsity team meeting due to his mature ability to compete, stood up and said, "I didn't come here to lose. I came here to win a state championship, so that's what I want. To win it all!"

You could have heard a pin drop, and I just let the silence fester to see how the others would react. Some of the older boys whispered to each other things that were not audible to the rest of us but inferred things like, "Doesn't he know where he is? There are private schools in our division now, and nobody beats the private schools."

There stood a courageous freshman who had not been tainted with the disbelief of the rest of the team and the townspeople. The discussion had now shifted to what I wanted to talk about in the first place, but it had to come from them, not me or the coach. I knew they could win. The coach knew they could win. And, apparently one freshman believed they could win. However, now we needed to see if the whole team could realistically get on the same page.

I thanked the young man for having the audacity to declare such a thing as winning the state championship. Then I turned to the rest of the team and asked, "How many of you would like the feeling that would come from winning a state championship?" They all raised their hands, and I was grateful we were now breaking created barriers little by little.

I continued, **"When you lose your excuses, you'll find your results.** How many of you honestly feel it is possible? If so, stand up!" The freshman who started the motion stood up first. Then slowly but surely, one by one the whole team was on their feet. Then I turned and looked at the coaches who were also now standing in the corner and said, "Gentlemen, allow me to present to you your state championship team." Applause and cheering broke out in the small room, along with enthusiastic high-fives. One of the players went over to the white board and wrote, "State Champions!!!" A false belief had been shattered in that little room, and they were ready for the next step, a shift in their language. The room had calmed down, and I expressed my confidence that they could in fact win, and it was also the only way to change the belief of the community. Now all that was left was the work.

I instructed them on the power of words. "The victory will first come in the mind. Then you must speak it as a team. I will now leave you in the hands of your coaches to come up with a list of affirmations. These affirmations must be memorized and said all together in unison before every practice, before every game, and individually before you go to bed at night. Are you all committed to do this!?"

A hardy and dedicated "Yes" left everyone in attendance with no doubt.

The Team did as they were instructed, and I was impressed with what they created. Imagine these boys in a circle with locked arms swaying side to side, increasing their volume as they confidently declared before every practice and every game:

The Team Affirmations

- It's our destiny to Win the State Championship.
- Winning comes naturally to us.
- State champions is in our blood.
- No one fights for Victory as hard as we do.
- We come together to pull off big Wins.
- We are NEVER out of any game, regardless of the score.
- **FOCUS** is one of our greatest strengths.
- Doubt is not welcome on our team.
- Our love for the game and our teammates is apparent. Nothing comes between us.
- We speak with our game and total domination on the court, not with arrogant comments.
- We understand that "Good Things happen to Good People," and we live our lives that way.
- Our quest is to change Basketball History at our school.
- Mark the date February 24th, **State Champions!!!**
- We Visualize that day, that moment, and that feeling!

I was enthralled that this team came up with affirmations to progress them in life as well, and not just to win basketball games. "We understand that good things happen to good people, and we live our lives that way." They went about playing with respect, honor, humility, and integrity as they declared, "We speak with our game and total domination on the court, not with arrogant comments."

That reminds me of something the author C. S. Lewis noted: **"Humility is not thinking less of yourself, it's thinking of yourself less."**

I later learned there had been some animosity between

two players because they happened to be interested in the same girl. On the court they were cordial, but off the court, not so much. This obviously had to change if these players were to be true champions, so they came up with, "Our love for the game and our teammates is apparent, nothing comes between us."

You are probably wondering what happened, aren't you? Well, their success didn't happen overnight. Just like anything, it took some consistent effort and dedication. The first year of putting this into place their record was 7 seven wins and five losses. They made it to the third round of the playoffs and lost in a nail-biter by one point.

As is common for athletes in a small town, many of the team also played football. I was made aware that affirmations were set as a football team, and they actually ended up winning the state championship in football that next year. One of the players, who started on both the football and basketball teams, told me he set personal affirmations in addition to the team affirmations. He was amazed that every single personal goal he affirmed daily came to fruition. Remarkable!

The next year, the basketball team declared the same affirmations before every practice and every game. They ended up with eleven wins and two losses and made it to the state championship finals, beating a private school in the playoffs. They came up short in the final, but the victory had nothing to do with the score. They had overcome the limiting belief that they couldn't even make it that far.

The third year, with much of the same team using the same winning language habits, they went undefeated with twelve wins and no losses in their section. They again made it to the state finals unscathed. The private school that had beaten them in the finals the year before got knocked out in an earlier round by another team. Here it was: they were to face another private school in the finals. The private school's point guard was the smallest guy in the starting line-up, and he was 6'1". It looked like a battle between David and Goliath. Most of the opposing team's starting line-up had already committed to major universities to play at the next level. Nonetheless, this little team from a small town in southeast Arizona went out and performed like champions, just like they said they would.

At the end of regulation play it was tied and the game went into overtime. At the end of the first overtime, they were neck and neck, and the game went into second overtime. In the end, a star player from the opposing team made a clutch shot and won the game. Although the score didn't reflect it, these boys and this town had won the greater triumph. They truly "changed basketball history at their school" and felt they could compete against any school, private or not.

I often reflect on the life lessons these boys learned at an early age as a result of saying these winning affirmations daily. Now they know they can win at anything they want, and so can anyone reading this book. The body and environment obey anything we tell them. There is no filter. If I say, "We can win," my body, mind, and spirit set out to achieve it. Likewise if I say, "We can't win," everything sets out to accomplish that end.

Saying what you want daily is the last and key step to Napoleon Hill's achievement formula explained in his classic *Think and Grow Rich.* It is the step that most people fail to take, and thus they fail to achieve what they want. Without the final step of repeating daily that which you specifically desire, it will rarely come to pass. I speak as a witness that this formula works. I have proven it many times over.

{Power Paragraph}

{It is key to write your daily affirmations as if you have already accomplished them. Starting with "I AM" statements is more powerful than "I want." Be a winner. Write down your desired accomplishments, and who you are, and verbally repeat those daily! **You will become and bring about what you affirm.}**

Write Down Seven Daily Winning Affirmations:

1. _____

   _____

2. _____

   _____

3. _____

   _____

4. _____

   _____

5. _____

   _____

6. _____

   _____

7. _____

   _____

Chapter 12

Words of Integrity

I put my pen down, walked over to the hotel window, and gazed out at the famous San Antonio River Walk. I could hear the boat tour guide on his loudspeaker entertaining those aboard. I observed the people passing each other and wondered how their rates of vibration were with their greetings. I pondered if this book, now almost completely written, would make a difference in those who decided to read and apply it.

I returned to the hotel desk and closed the leather-bound book, now a treasure to me, and took out Dr. Maxwell Wright's notes. I methodically glanced over each page that had given me direction in my writing. I gratefully reflected on how each chapter came together, except for the glaring vacancy where page 9 should be. Whatever it contained is a mystery; further, Clem said it alone had the ability to spark another movement.

Without warning, a courageous desire inspired me to retrieve page 9 from whomever took it. Somehow these antagonists "with accents" kept showing up in my path, and now I felt the responsibility to face them. They took something that was destined to be mine, something that contained the stimulus for another movement, and I intended to reclaim it. There was no sign of them so far here in San Antonio, but I had no doubt they would show up again.

I stood up to gather my things before I had to head to the airport. I noticed I had left page 8 out on the side of the desk, so I picked it up to put it with the others. As I held the page in my fingers I noticed it seemed to be thicker than the other pages. I brushed my thumb along the side of the old parchment and discovered another piece of paper stuck to it. I separated the two sheets and saw something very peculiar written at the top of the discovered sheet. There was no page number, but these undecipherable words were written on it: *"Worte der Integrität - die Gefahr der unverbindlichen Sprache"*

I sat back down at the hotel desk wondering what those words meant. I opened my laptop and typed into my search browser *worte der integritat* in English. The result showed that the phrase was German, and meant **"Words of Integrity."** I re-played how *worte der integrität* was pronounced in German several times on my computer. Then I inserted the rest of the phrase—*die gefahr der unverbindlichen sprache*. The English translation revealed **"The Danger of Non-Committal Language."** I looked back at the handwritten phrase and realized that it was not in Dr. Wright's handwriting. Someone else had written those words, and for some reason it was stuck to the back of page 8.

I contemplated what to do with this new-found page. Should I call Clem and let him know? Should I include this in the book? Regardless, now was not the time to try to figure it out, as I needed to start making my way down to the hotel lobby to catch the shuttle to the airport. So I packed the new-found page in a different folder apart from Dr. Wright's notes and headed out.

While waiting for the elevator to reach my floor, I noticed Dan Gable was approaching from down the hall. It was apparent he had just come from the hotel gym—he had a towel around his neck and was visibly sweaty. I took advantage of the situation and stepped out to greet him.

"Hi, Mr. Gable. Thank you for your inspired talk today," I said.

"Of course! I love talking to other champions," he replied confidently.

"How was your workout?" I asked.

"Pretty good, although I didn't hit my goal. You know, I've worked out every single day for as long as I can remember, and I still have yet to hit my goal," Dan complained as he took the towel from around his neck and started twisting it with intensity.

"Wow, what exactly is your goal Mr. Gable?"

"That I work out so hard, so intensely, that I pass out unconscious. Unfortunately, it still hasn't happened yet," he divulged with a hint of sarcasm, yet I had no doubt he was serious.

I was suddenly at a loss for words. How could I respond to this five-foot-nine He-Man who stood before me? All I could come up with was, "Sorry to hear that. I certainly wish you the best on reaching your goal my friend. Just hang in there, and I'm sure you'll pass out someday." He smiled at my making light of the situation. We shook hands as he continued walking down the hall.

For some reason, after talking to Dan, I felt like a wimp taking the elevator down to the lobby. Sure, I had my suitcase and super heavy computer bag that would justify taking the elevator, right? With a surge of fitness-based inspiration, I made my way to the stairwell with my bags held in the air as I descended five stories. My goal was different than Dan's, though. I just wanted to make it to the lobby in one piece.

"Mission accomplished!" I congratulated myself as I popped open the door to the ornate lobby.

"Thomas . . . Thomas Blackwell? Is that you?" I heard my name but couldn't see who was saying it. Then a dear old friend from high school was standing right in front of me.

"Jason Jackson, so good to see you my friend! How incredible are you!?" I asked.

"Not too bad, not too bad at all," Jason countered innocently, obviously not having read Chapter 5 about the rate of vibration of our daily greetings.

"What brings you to San Antonio, Amigo?" I inquired.

"Oh, I have a medical conference for orthopedic surgeons here this weekend. But I still live in Arizona," he answered. "And you?"

"Wow, you're an orthopedic surgeon? That's remarkable, Jason—or Dr. Jackson, rather," I congratulated. "I too am here for a conference, but now I'm heading home to Virginia," I explained.

"Well, hey, we should totally get together next time you are in Arizona and do lunch or something. Or maybe our families can get together and have a barbeque," Jason concluded as he was stepping away, inching his way from the hotel lobby back to his conference.

Out of the blue it was as if I had pushed the replay button on my computer another time, because in my mind, I heard the electronic German voice say, *Worte der integrität.*

Why had his invitation to get together next time I was in Arizona caused my stomach to turn? Then it hit me with undeniable force. **"Words of Integrity, the Danger of Non-Committal Language,"** I muttered at a level only I could hear. This situation was exactly what those words were referring to. Jason said we should get together next time I'm in Arizona, yet I don't even have his phone number. It's as if he was saying that just to be cordial, and to let me know we were still friends. He really had no intention of getting together with me, let alone my family. I realized this was not something just Jason did; many people do this. I've even done this! We throw around invitations with no commitments and no intention to be committed.

I returned to the present moment, resolving to write a chapter on the words of integrity and determined from that moment forward to be committed.

I hurried over to the conference room to catch my friend before he entered. "Jason, Jason, hold on . . . I need your cell phone number so I can let you know when I'm in Arizona," I beckoned.

Caught a little caught off guard, at my insistence he fumbled, "Of course, of course."

"I apologize, Thomas, I never even asked what you do," Jason considerately queried.

"I'm actually an author and a speaker, and I'm just about to finish a book on the power of our language and how we bring about what we talk about." I explained.

"Wow, fascinating. You'll have to send me a link so I can buy it when it's done," he said.

"Oh, I definitely will. Now that I have your cell number," I confirmed. "Actually, Jason, this just came to my mind regarding the chapter I'm writing right now. Would you mind helping me with a quick experiment?"

"As long as it doesn't hurt, I'm game," he agreed with a wink.

"You deal with joints and ligaments all the time in your medical profession, so I'm sure you'll like this. I've learned that our physical body responds to what we tell it and the words we speak. For example if you say, 'I can,' the body is strengthened. If you say, 'I can't,' then it obeys and falls weak. There is no filter system; our body and environment only know to respond to what we command," I expounded.

Dr. Jackson stood there without speaking, attempting to wrap his educated medical mind around what I just said. I could sense his skepticism, so I had no choice but to show him.

"Here, let me demonstrate this to you. Hold out your right arm. I am going to put some pressure on it with my whole hand, but I want you to resist and not let me push your arm down. I see that you can resist me, which is good. You must be working out," I mused. "Okay, so now I want you to say 'I can' and I want you to resist me pushing you down. Let's see if you have more strength than when I pushed down with no words."

He did as I asked, and I was not able to budge his arm this time. "Did you notice an increase in strength?" I inquired.

"Yes, I actually did," he responded.

"Okay, now I want you to resist me again, but this time I want you to say the opposite: 'I can't.' We'll see if your body responds."

Jason, still a little skeptical, said those debilitating words as I pressed down on his arm. Sure enough, I brought his arm down with ease. "Wait, wait, there's no way! Do it again," he requested.

"I'd be happy to, especially for your sake," I complied. Then once again as he said 'I can't,' he was left with no ability to hold up his arm.

"Wow, how did you do that? I totally felt a shift in my strength just by saying 'I can't,' Jason enthused.

"Not only that, but without telling you, when I couldn't budge your arm I was using my whole hand, and when I brought you down the last two times I was only using two fingers," I confessed. "You should also know that all positive words will sustain you, and all negative words will NOT sustain you."

To prove it to him we went through several more examples of words like *love* and *hate*. He was definitely a believer after that.

You would have thought we would have attracted more attention from onlookers in the lobby, but with a hotel full of orthopedic surgeons, me pressing down on Jason's arm to test his mobility appeared totally normal.

"All right, Dr. Jackson, that was just the education part, but not the real experiment I wanted to attempt with you. There are some words that are often said that relate to a person's commitment and to their ability to carry out the task at hand. I've not done this before, meaning I have not had someone say these next words while I attempt to push their arm down."

"What words are those?" my doctor friend asked curiously.

I paused for a moment to reflect on how I would explain. "Well, these words are declared so often, and are what I call 'non-committal words.' And, I believe it has contributed to a plaguing epidemic of a non-committal society. What we really want to know is if a person can be counted on, can be trusted, and are going to do what they say they are going to do."

"So c'mon, what are the words?" he questioned impatiently.

"The words are **'I think I can,' 'I'll try,' and 'I hope I can**.' Now, I honestly don't know what's going to happen, but I am highly curious. So, how about we see how the body responds to these words?"

Jason held out his right arm once again, and I instructed, "I want you to respond to my request by saying, 'I'll do it' while you resist me pushing down on your arm with my whole hand. Okay?"

"Okay, got it."

"Let's begin. Jason, I want you to resist me pushing down on your arm," I commanded.

"I'll do it!" he declared, and he withheld my force. He was immovable.

"Now respond with, 'I think I can.'"

He compliantly obeyed by saying "I think I can," and I dropped his arm very easily with my two fingers. We continued with him saying "I'll try" and "I hope I can," and the results were the same. I was able to push his arm down with two fingers and minimal effort. The body treated those non-committal phrases just the same as when a person says, "I can't." The results of the experiment demonstrated the danger in those words.

I continued, "Jason, imagine you are working with a patient in the recovery stages after surgery. How often do they say or think these weak words?"

"A lot more than they should, and now I've witnessed the power of it. **Our bodies and environment verifiably don't respond to 'I'll try,' 'I think I can,' or 'I hope I can.'** That was truly amazing Thomas! You let me know when your book is published, and moving forward, I am going to buy a copy for all the doctors in my department, and for all my patients. This will help their healing processes and their overall perspectives on life," he concluded.

"All right, my friend, that is very kind of you. Great to see you again, and thank you for your help with that experiment. I'll look forward to connecting again when I'm in Arizona," I said as we parted ways.

I caught the next shuttle to the airport and was once again excited to be heading home. While on the plane, I took out the piece of paper with the handwritten German text and determined to write a chapter on words of integrity, keeping it separate from the rest of the book.

I was fortunate to sit next to a four-year-old boy on the plane, and he helped me with some insight. I had just written on the page, "Where did this non-commitment language come from? When did it start?" Finding the origin of words can often help us get to the root of the issue. My answer came as this innocent little boy pulled out a well-known book about a talking train attempting to climb a mountain while saying "I think I can, I think I can. . . ." Had the little train just changed its language to **"I know I can,"** there's no doubt it would have had more strength and claimed victory over the hill a lot sooner.

I recalled a story that a previous mentor relayed to me that further illustrates the point.

An army sergeant is standing at the base of a hill with one of his soldiers. The sergeant gives a simple and direct command: "Soldier, I want you to take that hill."

The soldier replies to his sergeant with a salute, "I'll try, Sir!"

The sergeant, not satisfied, repeats, "Private, I want you to take that hill right now."

This time, a little confused, the private firmly responds, "I'll do my best, Sir!"

Now the sergeant, beginning to lose patience, shouts for a third-time, "Soldier, you take that hill now, and I mean it!"

Not understanding the dilemma, the soldier again responds, "I think I can, Sir."

Fed up with the lack of commitment, the sergeant turns to another soldier and gives the same command. The response was music to his ears as the new soldier replied, "Yes, Sir, **I will do it!**"

{Power Paragraph}

{Some of the weakest words in the human language are, "I'll try." Instead of just "trying," why not **decide to get it done?** People say "I'll try" as a disclaimer just in case the desired result is not produced. When we are asked to accomplish a task and we respond with, "I'll do my best," there is hesitation and a lack of confidence. In the Bible, Jesus teaches, "But let your communication be yea, yea; nay, nay: for whatsoever is more than these cometh of evil." Could it be that non-commitment comes from an evil source? Is it true that this evil source is pleased with the lack of commitment in our language and actions? We have become accustomed to and accepting of a non-committal language. That has produced a non-committal society with non-committal results. If you say you are going to do it, then do it. If you say you're going to be there, then be there. If you cannot complete the task, then say so. Either way, **Just Do It!**

Enough with the wishy-washy mentality and language. Change your language, change your commitment level.}

When it comes to integrity, the main questions are, "Can you be counted on?" and "Can you be trusted to do what you say you will do?" What people say and what they do are often two separate things. Let me explain this with the following Integrity Graph.

Integrity Graph

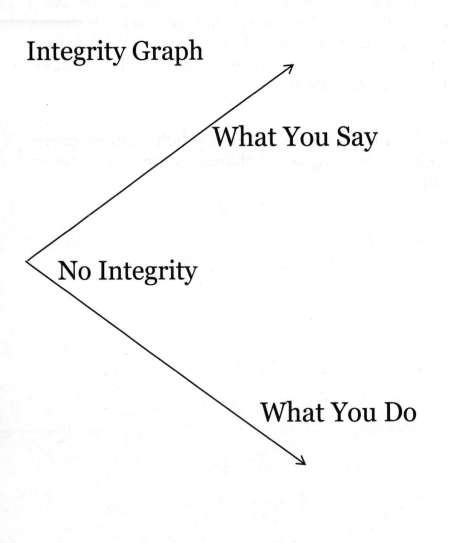

Do What You Say, and Say What You Do!

= Integrity

Chapter 13

The Final Report

and

The Next Movement

Once again early December was upon us, and I could hardly believe it had already been almost a year since I first went to Boston. I had finished writing chapters that coincided with the notes in the leather-bound book except for the additional chapter on "Words of Integrity." That one was written on the separate page beneath the German title I found stuck to page 8.

Prior to our meeting, Clem had requested that I send him the leather-bound book and all of Dr. Wright's notes in a secure package so he and his father could review what I had written. I did so, but for some reason I was hesitant to send the added chapter on integrity. I determined to keep that one in my possession and to present it to them personally at the hotel in Boston in about a week.

My family and I began to carry out our cherished holiday traditions. One favorite tradition among many is what we call our "thankful chain." The week of Thanksgiving we take several small strips of paper and fill each one with something or someone we are thankful for. Then we glue them all together, forming a massive chain that we hang somewhere visible in our home throughout the Christmas season. One important detail to note about this tradition is that before we glue each piece of the chain, the item of gratitude is read to the whole family. This always creates a wonderful feeling in our home. After writing the chapter on gratitude, thankfulness, and appreciation, it all makes more sense now.

Feelings of love and gratitude in our home are something we are constantly working on, so having these traditions sure helps. Although the thankful chain helps boost our holiday spirits, we have another daily tradition that helps us stay on track throughout the year. We initiated this practice during the thirteen days of our little angel baby's life. Each day and for the entire day, someone is assigned to say all the family prayers. This typically consists of morning prayer, blessings on the food we partake, and evening prayer prior to going to bed. After the evening prayer, the person who prayed during the day gets to be in the spotlight as each of the other family members say what they love about that person. This ensures that any and all feelings of contention that might have crept in throughout the day are dispelled from among us and from our home. It has also built stronger loving relationships between us. This takes consistent effort, just like anything of worth and value.

The time came for me to go back to Boston and report to Clem and his father. Kimberly and the girls took me to the airport just like they had a year ago. I stood on the curb, giving each of my girls a hug and a kiss.

"I believe in you. I always have," Kimberly said as she bid me farewell.

I silently offered a prayer for the protection of my family

while I was away. I also prayed that everything would come together amazingly in meeting with Clem and his father.

When I arrived at the Boston airport and saw all its same holiday décor and energy, it made the year that had passed feel like it was just a month. On the other hand, so much had happened. So many things had changed. I had certainly changed, and a sudden feeling of inadequacy fell over me as I remembered the congratulatory note I received after winning the speech contest. I found a secluded chair at the airport, pulled out the note, and read it again.

"A chance to change the world . . ." I said to myself. This was the part about which I felt inadequate. The world is a big place, and I hardly felt that I had scratched the surface. Maybe changing the world had more to do with page 9?

Just thinking about the stolen page caused me to be on guard, but now I was determined to get it back. The people who had conspired to steal it were no longer looking for me—*I* was looking for *them*. And I was certain they were close by.

I popped up from my chair and walked through the baggage claim, to the exit, and toward the taxi line. I scanned the area but did not spot anyone that fit the "bad guy" profile.

"The old Charles Street jail please," I instructed the taxi driver.

"You got it," he said with a heavy Boston accent.

The day was clear and sunny, and the trees were already barren from an early November freeze. While riding in the back seat, I noticed an executive car that had been behind us through every twist and turn in our route. The windows were tinted so darkly I couldn't see the occupants, but something felt suspicious.

"You know what, I just had a change of plans. Can you take me to the North End? The Italian District, please," I abruptly told the driver. If this car was in fact following us, a simple detour would reveal it.

"You got it," he replied.

The executive car still, close behind, continued to follow us all the way to the North End. It had to be them.

"These friends of yours?" the taxi driver caught me off guard.

"I'm sorry, what was that?" I questioned

"These people in the car behind us, trailing me like I have a bag of gold. Are they friends of yours?" He repeated.

"You noticed them following us too?" I continued

"Of course, I'm a professional driver, it's what I do. I notice everything on the road around me," the taxi driver said with confidence.

It was the moment of decision. I could be scared, or I could embrace the fact that I had these guys exactly where I wanted them.

"Yes, they are friends of mine; in fact we all decided to just go back to the hotel. Would you mind heading back there?" I requested.

"You got it!" he repeated, for the third time.

After he said, "You got it," I appreciated his style, because it sounded like, "Yes Sir, I'll do it!" I liked this guy's ability to speak with integrity.

As we approached the hotel and pulled in to the drop-off area, the executive car did not follow suit; instead, its driver kept on driving right past the front entrance. They now knew I was here, and though I did not know my next move, I trusted all things would work out somehow.

"Mr. Blackwell, welcome back!" It was the same bell captain I had met the year before. "You weren't kidding; you said you'd be back in a year, and here you are," he said with an impressive memory.

"Hi there, friend, what a remarkable memory you have," I complimented.

"How's that speed reading coming along?"

"I've done my share of it over the past year, and a bit of speed writing too!" I retorted with no further explanation.

As I went up the escalator, I glanced over at the lower level restaurant, remembering that crazy night where this all started. I noticed the doors to the ballroom were open, and I was lured into peeking inside. It was empty, so I walked around a bit and reminisced about the anxious and blissful feelings from the speech contest just twelve months before.

A sealed envelope was given to me at the registration desk, and I made my way up to my room. Before entering, I made sure no one was following me, and locked my door once inside. I was curious about the letter, so I went to the desk and opened it.

Dear Thomas, You made it. Congratulations! The material you have written in the book is remarkable, well done! Clem and I look forward to meeting you tonight in "the basement" at 11:00 p.m. sharp.

Night arrived quickly, and the restaurants were now closing. I hung out in the lobby inconspicuously, every once in a while glancing toward the restaurant entrance to see when I could enter undetected. The cooks closing down the kitchen were making a considerable amount of noise, and the hostess was no longer at her station. This was my chance. I made my way to the third jail cell and moved the table away from the metal door just as Clem and I had done last December. I entered the escape hatch without being seen. The musky odor once again filled my senses as I climbed down the ladder and carefully replaced the metal door. I could see a light and hear talking at the end of the hallway in the same room where I had been given the leather-bound book and Dr. Maxwell Wright's notes. Those positive phrases written on the walls had a lot more significance in my life now. I spotted Clem, who was waiting at the door to the room to greet me.

Clem and his father were huddled in the small room, which was lighted by a battery-powered camping light. "Thomas, my friend, so we meet again," he cheerfully said as he embraced me with a manly hug. "You remember my father, Max, from the contest, right?"

"I do, it's great to finally know your name, by the way. Up until now, you've just been 'Clem's father.'"

Max held the book and notes in his left hand and began the conversation. "First off, let me congratulate you for finishing the book, and quite impressively elaborating on all the notes as you created each chapter. This was no small task, but you've done it. There is nothing we would change, and before he died my father, Dr. Maxwell Wright, instructed us not to change anything once it was written. This book will be published and go out to the world in many languages," Max explained.

"Do you have any further questions for us, Thomas?" Clem chimed in.

"Actually, I do. There are a lot of unanswered questions and strange situations that have transpired since last year. For example, there are people who know about me and about this book. They've been following me, and one of them ran off with page 9. What is on page 9?" I asked in a concerned tone.

Suddenly we heard the echo of the metal door open and close. We all froze as we heard multiple footsteps make their way down the hall. Clem and I hurried into a dark corner of the room, attempting to not be seen. Max held his ground and did not budge from his place, clearly to be discovered in the light.

"Dad, get over here, they'll see you!" Clem whispered with intensity.

Just then, the figure of a man stood in the doorway. "Hello, Max," an older man said with that now-familiar foreign accent. His face was in the shadows, yet he looked familiar to me. He was soon flanked by two younger-looking men, blocking our potential escape.

Clem and I remained in the shadows of the corner not wanting to be seen. My heart was pounding, and I could sense the animosity in Clem as well.

The man peered over to the corner where we stood, obviously figuring out our whereabouts and said, "And, hello Mr. Blackvell. Vee meet again."

The hair stood up on the back of my neck as this mysterious man said my name. I stepped closer to him to get a better look. Sure enough it was Friedrich the German man I met in Tucson. And wait, how did he know Max already?

"You remember my two sons, Johan and Andreas, don't you Mr. Blackvell?" Friedrich mused. I certainly recognized one of them as the fake chauffeur in Las Vegas.

"Hello Friedrich, what are you doing here?" Max asked.

Just then, Clem revealed his presence from the shadows. "Hold on, who are you and how do you know my father?" "Dad, you know this person?" Clem asked in frustration.

Max looked at Clem in silence and nodded his head, acknowledging he did in fact know Friedrich.

"I thought we had an agreement, Friedrich," Max continued.

"Vee did Max, and vee schtill do. Vee vere goink to let you choose zee author through your shpeech contest and zen let him go and shpeak. Vee agreed zat vee vould observe him in his shpeeches and make zure he met our approval," Friedrich expounded.

Then Friedrich's attention was turned to me, and his demeanor softened a bit. "Let me say congratulations to Thomas, as he has far exceeded our lofty expectations. Zere is no doubt he is zee right man to take zis message to zee world."

I was grateful for the praise, but still quite shocked with the whole situation. I glanced over at Clem with a look that demanded to know if he knew anything about this agreement with Friedrich. Clem quickly shook his head and shrugged his shoulders, attempting to wipe his hands clean of the newfound information.

Max spoke again with a level of frustration. "Then what's the problem, and where did this go wrong? This was just supposed to be an observation, but then your boys starting going after Thomas trying to get the notes!"

Friedrich responded with a low, steady tone. "Yes, Max, but zis vas before vee knew zat my fazer, Heinrich, who shpent time in jail wis your fazer, Dr. Wright, and helped dig out zis place, had also helped contribute to zis language movement. In his journal before he died, my fazer noted zat he had started an important facet of our language zat vas going to be a schapter in zee book, and zat he wrote it in zee notes. So vee vanted to see vat zat vas and set out to get it from Thomas."

Clem joined his father and started sifting through the notes, shaking their heads to indicate that nothing in the notes alluded to Heinrich writing anything down. Meanwhile, Friedrich and his two sons began to discuss something intensely in German, and I was standing there caught in the middle of all of it. Then I heard those familiar German words come out of Andreas's mouth: "*Worte der integrität.*"

"Words of integrity," I said softly, but no one heard me in the midst of all their arguing. "Words of integrity!" I shouted. All the attention was on me now. I carefully pulled out the page of notes to which they were referring, and that I had neatly folded to fit in my back pocket.

"Here is the page where your father, Heinrich, wrote, *Worte der integrität.* It means 'words of integrity,' and he also wrote the danger of non-committal language. I found it stuck to the back of page 8 when I was in San Antonio. It was written in German and I could tell it was not Dr. Maxwell Wright's handwriting, so I figured someone else had written it. I took the liberty to write another chapter on the subject, and here it is on this page," I explained.

Friedrich approached me with solemnity and asked, "Can I see vere my fazer wrote zose vords?"

"Yes, and I would like to include this in the book, if you are all okay with that," I told Friedrich and his two sons. "Also, I believe you have something of ours. I'd like to get back page 9."

Friedrich motioned back to Johan, and he pulled out page 9 from his coat pocket. We mutually exchanged the two notes, and their attention turned to looking over what I had written while I approached Max and Clem with the ransomed page 9.

"Max, would you like to do the honors and read what your father wrote?" I invited.

Max carefully unfolded the paper and began to scan over the page. Friedrich and his sons looked up in anticipation, even though they were already very aware of what was written on page 9—having had it in their possession for the last twelve months. Of all the notes, it appeared to be the longest Dr. Wright had written based on Max's extensive silent reading and unspoken interpretation.

"It really is quite remarkable. My father, Dr. Wright, was undeniably ahead of his time when he created this. This is absolutely another movement, and perhaps a whole other book needs to be written. I can see how parents, our school systems, universities, companies, and anyone in a leadership position, just to name a few, would greatly benefit from this knowledge," Max commented. Then he handed page 9 to Clem—while I still remained in the dark regarding its mysterious contents.

Clem carefully read the last page in silence as we all patiently waited to hear his feedback. "Remarkable is right. Anyone with the responsibility to speak to a group, teach a class, lead or coach a team, or manage an organization needs to hear this," Clem said as he handed page 9 back to his father.

"Needs to hear what?" I eagerly asked.

Max turned to me and read only the top portion of page 9. "I. M. I. The next great movement after one changes their language." Then he confidently placed the page in my hands. "I am going to let you read the rest of it when you are alone."

Max looked over to Friedrich and his sons, who seemed less hostile now. He then glanced at Clem and nodded, which caused Clem to nod as well as if to agree to something.

"Well, Thomas, it looks like you have another book to write. Are you up to the challenge?" Max asked as he handed me page 9.

"Whoa, I just finished this one. Now you want me to write another one?" I asked.

"That's what we're saying, Mr. Blackwell. You've proven you can handle it, and you've figured out how to inspire people. So, it's all yours!" Clem's father answered.

Friedrich handed me the page on words of integrity. "Vee agree, Thomas, and you have proven yourself. Zat next movement is crucial right now. Also, vee have looked over zis schapter on vords of integrity, and vee trust vat you've written to be a great addition to *Zee Liberty of Our Language Revealed*."

"Thank you, Friedrich. I appreciate your approval," I said.

Max soberly took the leather-bound book, now complete, held it in both hands, and put it against his chest. A fulfilled smile crossed his lips as he took in a deep breath. He brushed his right thumb across the inspiring notes written by his father that were nestled in the back of the book, then proceeded to gently flip through the chapters I created as a result. He appeared to be reflecting on his own journey, that of being charged with the knowledge about the basement and holding a speech contest for several years until finding the author and mouthpiece. Finally, Max spoke in a solemn tone, "So, Thomas, now that you've written *The Liberty of Our Language Revealed*, congratulations on changing the whole world."

"I have to be honest, gentlemen. I really don't feel like I've even made a dent, so how would I attempt to author another movement?" I expressed with concern.

Then Friedrich with his two sons stood next to Max and Clem so they were all facing me together. "Has your vorld changed as a result of changing your language?" Friedrich asked.

"Yes, of course. Tremendously. By leaps and bounds!" I acknowledged.

"How has it changed your world?" Max asked.

I began to reflect on each chapter, and how each one helped shape my life for the better. I paused and looked around the room in which we were standing, and the place where it all began. Winning the speech contest with a hope to embark on a new career. Clem and Max trusting me to write the book. And, of course, my experiences.

A sense of emotion came over me as I realized everything that had happened for me in the last year. In a bit of a choked-up voice I began, "I now know that when we greet people we have the power and ability to raise our rate of vibration and reap the effects of being in a higher state. I have put this into practice. I've witnessed firsthand what happens to our physical bodies and environment when we choose heavenly words instead of negative devilish words. The dark side will never sustain us.

"I know the effects of speaking to people with love and kindness and 'shining their divine sign.' Attitudes of once hostile people changed from an enemy to a friend right in front of me. I now know and have implemented my sense of appreciation for life and all that I have. I feel my personal value has increased, and I've actually been sleeping a lot better as a result of constantly being in a state of gratitude," I continued.

Again, my emotions were on the surface as I thought of my experience with Poppy and Helen in Tucson and speaking at Patrick's funeral. I started in again with a more reverent tone. "Forgiveness, both asking for it and granting it to others, adds life to our days. It is one of the most liberating acts we can experience. I know the power of language when it comes to money matters. There is no limit in our ability to accumulate wealth and abundance, only limits in our language and beliefs."

I pictured sitting down with Rudy and sitting in the exclusive audience with Dan Gable. "I learned that those who win in any endeavor **simply say they can** and go for it. Champions are born by first speaking who they are into existence."

I glanced over to my new German friends and said, "And I now know, and have implemented, words of integrity. I do what I say, and I say what I do. I can be counted on. There is no more non-committal language in my vocabulary."

I purposefully made eye contact with each of the five men in the partially lit escape route who graciously listened to me. Finally, Clem stepped forward and broke the prolonged silence.

"Then the whole world has changed, Thomas. YOUR whole world," Clem stated.

Max elaborated, "We all see the world through our own eyes and perceptions. If you want to change the world, simply change your perception of it. **Our language is a manifestation of our perceptions.**"

Then Friedrich chimed in, "So, if you help to schange just one person's language, to really undershtand zat zey bring about vat zey talk about, you've schanged zeir vorld. Thomas, you helped schange mine in Tucson, just by zee inspirational talk you gave on gratitude. Zee majority of my prayers now are expressing vat I am grateful for, and I'm even expressing gratitude for my schallenges."

"You helped schange my vorld ven you spoke to zose shtudent leaders on zee physical power of our vords. From zat day I have shtopped telling Andreas he vas ugly," Johan said jovially as we all had a hardy laugh. "Seriously, zough, I realized during your talk I had some sings I needed to schange in my life, especially vith my schoice of vords. Zey vere making me veak before, and now I know zat my physical body only responds to vat I say. So, sank you," Johan concluded.

Max approached, put his hand on my shoulder, looked me in the eyes, and said, "You see, Thomas, this movement changes the world one person at a time. Those who decide to implement what you've written will never be the same."

A sense of deeper understanding filled the room, as all eyes were on me anticipating my next words.

"That's right, my friends. I get it now. **Our world WILL CHANGE . . . if we SAY so!**

I felt satisfied and humbled with the book I had written, and at the same time I felt a surge of faith and confidence knowing the Lord would guide me on the next great movement. I looked at the men in front of me and declared, "Gentlemen, I will author the next movement."

"Wonderful, Mr. Blackwell, and we are all here to support your next journey however we can. How about we plan to meet here in the hotel basement in one year's time, so you can report on your progression," Max suggested.

I nodded in agreement as I approached Clem and Max to give them a parting handshake and a brotherly hug. With page 9 in my hand, I was now face to face with Friedrich, Johan, and Andreas. I extended my hand in friendship, "And I can take confidence knowing there will be no fake chauffeurs, right?"

The German father and his two sons all smiled and assured me only *real chauffeurs* from this point forward. I assertively made my way out of the small musky room with the others trailing a short distance behind me.

Once again, I took time to read all of the powerful words of wisdom etched on the walls of the old escape route. Just before ascending the old wooden ladder I peered over to the right and noticed the figure of a single letter carved into one of the bricks. I took out my cell phone to shed some light on it. Chills went down my spine as I noticed it was the letter *I*. Directly to the right of it on a separate brick was carved the letter *M*. Full of anticipation, I continued searching along the wall to see if there was another letter that signified the title of page 9. Then, sure enough, further to the right on another brick was the remaining *I*. I curiously reached out and ran my fingers against the old brick that contained the last letter. My heart began to pound as the brick unexpectedly slid into the wall. Suddenly, without warning, a loud clicking noise rang out and dust began to fill the hallway. I hurriedly stepped back from the old wooden ladder as I felt the ground begin to tremble a little. Once the dust finally settled, my eyes beheld a tiny door that had mysteriously opened directly behind the old wooden ladder.

I glanced back at the others to see if they noticed what was happening right before us. They were all frozen speechless, and their eyes wide with curious amazement. A rush of enthusiasm came over me. "Well, gentlemen, it looks like we have *revealed* some more material for the next great movement!"

Acknowledgments

My sincere gratitude goes out to so many who made this book and movement a possibility.

First, I want to give thanks to my Heavenly Father, who graciously provided the inspiration to write each chapter and who gave all of us the power to create our blessed lives through our words.

To my beautiful wife, Kimberly, my best friend, my confidant, and the one whose hand fits perfectly in mine to hold forever. To my precious daughters, Makayla, Charity, and Liberty May for believing in their Daddy, suggesting their candid ideas, and having patience.

To my sweet angel daughter Melody June, whose encouragement I felt spurring me on from the unseen world where angel babies go. Until we meet again.

Much appreciation to my parents, John and Annabel Hall, for believing in anything I say . . . especially you mom! You've always told me "I could," and it worked!

To my siblings, Kara, Brian, Wick, Garrett, and Ginger, for all the laughs and love over the years and for always providing me with good material.

Thank you to my friend and brilliant editor, Dr. C. Ryan Dunn. You've taught me the power of the formation of our language. You amaze me with your diligently achieved gifts.

Muchisimas gracias to David Bayer for writing a generous foreword and for being a genuine friend and mentor. I've learned to live in a "beautiful state" because of you.

To my book cover designer and website guru Jennifer Jedow. A sincere thank you for sharing your incredible expertise and for just being flat-out awesome!

A huge thank you to all those who took the time and energy to express their candid feedback for the book and for me personally. Among them: Lisa Nichols, Tom Ziglar, Duane Cummings, Rob Shallenberger, Nancy Matthews, Sean Greeley, Nicholas Loise, Dr. Andreas Boettcher, Davy Tyburski, Kevin Allen, Mark Brown, Eric English, Mike Crow, and Howard Partridge. You've all affected my life for the better!

About the Author

Thomas Blackwell is the CEO and Founder of **Say Do Achieve**, whose vision is to significantly improve the language and mindset of more than one billion people worldwide through authorship, inspirational talks and workshops, and peak performance coaching. He has given more than a thousand talks and workshops worldwide to corporations, executives, entrepreneurs, sales teams, athletes, religious groups, and students.

While attending Northern Arizona University on a music/voice scholarship, Thomas competed in tennis and soccer and later coached tennis at the Division I level. His business experience runs deep as he has owned and operated a successful seven figure insurance agency with more than one hundred agents in three different locations. While realizing some significant success in business in 2004 he was asked to tell his story in seven minutes to a group of more than ten thousand people. His being requested to speak and inspire as a keynote and facilitator has never stopped since. This inevitably led him to this vocation he didn't even know was an option.

Above it all, Thomas's greatest blessings from God are being married to his high school sweetheart, and being the father to four precious daughters.

*To request Thomas for a Keynote, Workshop Training, or Peak Performance Coaching go to:

www.SayDoAchieve.com

Look for Thomas's next books by staying connected . . .

Visit **www.SayDoAchieve.com** and sign up for Thomas's FREE Weekly Inspirational Language Tips and you will also receive the latest updates.

The Next Movement...

Instructional

Motivational

Inspirational

The Three Levels of
Effective
Speaking and Teaching

Thomas Blackwell